The Yankee Fleet

Maritime New England in the Age of Sail

James C. Johnston Jr.

Charleston · London
History PRESS

Published by The History Press
Charleston, SC 29403
www.historypress.net

Copyright © 2007 by James C. Johnston Jr.
All rights reserved

Cover image: Action between USS Constitution and HMS Guerriere, 19 August 1812, attributed to Thomas Birch. Painting in the collections of the U.S. Naval Academy Museum. Bequest of Mrs. Walter Jennings, 1949.

First published 2007

Manufactured in the United Kingdom

ISBN 978.1.59629.325.0

Library of Congress Cataloging-in-Publication Data

Johnston, James C., 1944-
The Yankee fleet : maritime New England in the age of sail / James C. Johnston, Jr.
p. cm.
Includes bibliographical references.
ISBN 978-1-59629-325-0 (alk. paper)
1. New England--History, Naval--17th century. 2. New England--History, Naval--18th century. 3. New England--History, Naval--19th century. 4. Seafaring life--New England--History. 5. Sailors--New England--Biography. 6. Pirates--New England--Biography. 7. New England--Biography. 8. United States. Navy--History. 9. United States--History, Naval. I. Title.
F4.J57 2007
974--dc22

2007029684

Notice: The information in this book is true and complete to the best of our knowledge. It is offered without guarantee on the part of the author or The History Press. The author and The History Press disclaim all liability in connection with the use of this book.

All rights reserved. No part of this book may be reproduced or transmitted in any form whatsoever without prior written permission from the publisher except in the case of brief quotations embodied in critical articles and reviews.

*This book is dedicated to my mother and best friend,
Clara J. Johnston, who has inspired in me a love of all things historic
and a passion for the sea.*

Contents

Chapter 1	The Lady Without Mercy	7
Chapter 2	The Voyage of the *Mayflower* and Her Sisters	21
Chapter 3	A Rover's Life	35
Chapter 4	More Depraved Pirates, Buccaneers and Henpecked Rovers	53
Chapter 5	Merchants and Bloody Americans Before the Revolution	69
Chapter 6	The Sailing Navy at War	83
Chapter 7	Eight Hundred Brave Americans A-whaling for to Go	107
Chapter 8	The American Century of Sail	133
Bibliography		155

Chapter 1

THE LADY WITHOUT MERCY

The primal forests spread down to the Atlantic Ocean in the northern portion of New England, and to the south, there were sand-covered shores. The beaches were the natural result of the action of wind, the churning of the mighty ocean and the warming and cooling of the earth's surface. Fine sands stretched out across the expanse of the littoral zone and beach. On other parts of the shoreline, where nature was to be less kind to the bare feet of the bathers who would come here in future times, were expanses of sea-polished and rounded stones. Here they carpeted the shore next to the breaking waves of the mighty Atlantic.

This great ocean was both a highway to a new life in an unexplored land and a great economic opportunity for people with vision, energy or just a lot of luck. This mighty ocean could also be a very hard mistress. She was both beautiful and hard to tame. Many foundering vessels had proven the truth of this hard fact. But there is one incontestable truth. The men who came to New England, and made it their own, had to come to terms with the sea, which was the source of their wealth and was to become the heritage of their blood. There was a bond between man and the sea that had to be clearly understood and appreciated. To sunder that bond could produce fatal consequences. That was the philosophical truth for all who dwelt along the shore and those who would board wooden ships and sail the deep. They knew this in their hearts from birth. The ocean gave up its riches, but it also exacted a high price from time to time in exchange for its favors.

Huge rocks are found on the shore, just as they were in ages past. They were deposited by the gigantic Pleistocene glaciers when they retreated about twelve thousand years ago. It was on one such monolithic behemoth, according to legend, that our Pilgrim fathers and mothers first set foot at Plymouth in New England. And we have enshrined that rock under a canopy of stone as "Plymouth Rock." For centuries to come, tourists would chip away at this souvenir until, for its own protection, it had to be enshrined under the protective canopy that we see today as it sits by the sea in the township of Plymouth, Massachusetts.

The Yankee Fleet

Early colonial whaling offshore.

The first people in New England were the Native Americans. They fished the Atlantic seas and had even taken whales offshore in the waters of the bay and on the surface of the wild Atlantic. That must have been a sight to see, in the glory days, when the bronzed Wampanoags and Gay Head Indians paddled their oceangoing canoes after the great right whales. Later on, other generations of Nantucket men, including some Native Americans, would chase the great whales all over the oceans of the world. These new European-born men, and their sons, and grandsons and great-grandsons, in turn would build towers on the beach to sight the whales, and then having seen them, they would take to their boats in chase. The hunt would lead them farther and farther away from the reassuring shoreline until they resolved to fit out larger vessels to better engage in the hunt of the whale to take his oil, bones and baleen. Eventually this activity would take them beyond the horizons and imagination of their more land-bound ancestors. They would smell the sea, take great draughts of it into their lungs and revel in it. It was as if they had found their true mother and their birthright in the deep waters of the Atlantic.

The first Europeans to sight the New England coast were most likely the Vikings. In the tenth century, these warriors, in their long dragon ships, settled in Iceland.

The Lady Without Mercy

Photograph of the Viking ship that was featured at the Columbian Exposition in 1893.

In 930 C.E., they established what many considered the first northern European parliament. It still meets to this day and has been called the Althing since the time of its inception. This rugged democracy dictated that Viking leaders were to be men chosen for their proven abilities and not always by their birth. The long ships that carried the Vikings from Scandinavia to Iceland, Greenland and eventually to North America were of lapped construction. These adventuring people of Scandinavia named the parts of this new country that they had discovered Markland and Vinland because of the great wealth of grapes found there. They aspired to colonize this land, but Native Americans would have other ideas about this.

The sides of the long ships were formed by overlapping strips of wood, which were then secured by iron nails. These ships were truly long and elegant, often reaching over a hundred feet in length. These wooden ships were oar propelled by men of iron constitution over thousands of miles of the northern oceans and fierce Atlantic by using the strength of their backs, as well as by a great sail which was rigged to the mast centered at the middle of the ship.

In the Old Norse sagas, we hear of Eric the Red who was banished for shedding aristocratic blood. He was forced to flee west over the deep waters of the unforgiving North Atlantic to Greenland toward the end of the tenth century to start life anew. These great sagas also tell the story of his son Leif who sailed west to discover new lands about 1000 C.E. These voyages in the open long ships of the Vikings must have been very cold and wet. If Viking women and children were aboard during a voyage, a cabin or some other shelter would be erected on the deck. These

Vikings were a hardy people who practiced a unique and savage ritual calculated to strengthen their race. When their children were born, they were taken by their fathers to ice-cold springs, soaked and then held aloft to the sky, naked to the winds and climate. Only the strongest babies would survive this ritual. After that rude introduction to Viking life, a soaking on an open ship on a stormy sea would not seem quite so challenging.

Other Vikings followed, pushing down into New England and even pushing inland into the area of what is now the town of Upton, Massachusetts. Here, about fifty miles from the salty shore, they built beehive-shaped huts. These huts were used by the Vikings during winters. Now, these distinctly Norse dwellings are under several feet of debris that has accumulated over the last thousand years. During a good part of the year, these huts are also underwater. I should note that these beehive-shaped shelters are on private property and access is not open to the public.

These beehive dwellings have been the source of a great deal of speculation, the subject of at least one book and several articles. We know that the Vikings attempted to colonize the northeastern portion of North America, but they discovered that the Native Americans were not willing to share living space with such an aggressive people as the wild Vikings. Nor were the Native Americans averse to defending themselves. A formidable foe, the Native Americans forced the Vikings to return to Greenland. Defeat in battle was new to the Norsemen. They didn't like it, and they did not choose to go back for more.

In four hundred years' time, nature itself turned on the Norsemen. What we now know as a mini ice age began in the 1300s. By 1438, even the rugged Norse in Greenland died of privation and the extreme cold. It is thought that their lack of adaptability to the ways of the native Greenlanders was their undoing, as it is commonly believed that their Christian religious leaders were in opposition to the native diet, which they held to be disgusting. This prejudice to all things native to Greenlanders had a great deal to do with the Europeans' ultimate demise. By 1438, only Iceland remained as the westernmost outpost of the Norse world.

In 1492 Italian navigator Christopher Columbus made the first of his four voyages of discovery to what became known as the New World. He sailed in the names of his patrons Queen Isabella and King Ferdinand of Spain. His discoveries would earn him a place in history as one of the greatest explorers and the greatest of risk takers. Of course his willingness to go on a voyage into the great unknown also carried its own rewards. Columbus dreamed of royal favor, fame, wealth and the titles of viceroy and "Admiral of the Ocean Seas." He didn't get all he wanted, but he did get a lot more out of life than most people who were raised in his non-aristocratic circumstances could ever have hoped for. His activities, and those of the conquistadors who followed him, are very well known and do not have to be retold here. Their ships brought glory and power to Spain, making it the world's dominate power for the better part of a hundred years.

The Lady Without Mercy

The *Santa Maria* as it appeared at the Columbian Exposition in 1893.

The energy of Columbus's Spanish masters was focused far to the south of New England in mineral-rich Central and South America as well as Mexico. The earliest explorers' ships were a marvel however. They were high-pooped carricks and caravels less than a hundred feet in length. They sailed well in the seas at hourly speeds of two to four knots. Speeds of four knots were rare for these vessels, but it could be done with a good wind if the bottom was clean of growth. From time to time, these early ships had to be hauled up onto the beach to have their bottoms scraped of plant and animal accumulations that had gathered up since their last cleaning. This process was called careening. Many an old wooden ship went down to Davy Jones's Locker for want of a cleaning. This sailor's task of cleaning, scraping and tarring a ship's bottom was essential to its survival. In centuries to come, some bright fellow hit on the idea of nailing copper sheets to the bottom of ships for protection from organic growth and the depredation of shipworms, which habitually ate the wooden planking. As Spain's empire grew, so did the size and quality of their ships. Great galleons replaced the smaller craft in the race for colonization as well as transportation of treasure.

It fell to another Italian navigator, who is best known by his English name, John Cabot, to explore the coast of Labrador, Newfoundland, and the area north of New England. Cabot, like so many Europeans, wanted to sail west in quest of fame

The *Nina* and the *Pinta* as they appeared at the Columbian Exposition in 1893.

and fortune. His problem was that he lacked the patrons to make it all possible. Like Columbus, he shopped around from royal court to royal court looking for this elusive patron. His quest led him to the court of one of England's most tightfisted monarchs, Henry VII. Henry VII had always been cautious about money and could only bring himself to pledge ten pounds to Cabot's venture. His royal approval was beyond price however, and the ten pounds he invested showed that it would be perfectly proper for others to invest in the venture as well.

Henry VII had come to England's throne after defeating Richard III at the Battle of Bosworth Field in 1485. This battle ended the feudal period of England's history and the dynastic Wars of the Roses. This victory of monarchy over feudalism had the effect of breaking the military power and influence of the armed English nobility and led to the rise of the middle class to economic and political power. In time, England would become the richest nation on earth, well founded on the modern concepts of trade. England, the nation of shopkeepers, would rule the commercial world and finance exploration. The merchants, influenced by the king's token approval of the venture, furnished Cabot with a ship, the *Matthew*, and supplied and crewed the vessel. Henry VII had truly shown them the way by his symbolic ten-pound investment in Cabot's voyage.

Cabot's ship had a high sterncastle and forecastle. It looked little different than the ships of Columbus. It was a sturdy vessel, and its sails carried Cabot to America

These proofs of the jubilee issue of Newfoundland in 1897 depict Henry VII; Cabot's ship, the *Matthew*; Cape Bonavista and John Cabot.

in 1497. This event was commemorated on a series of fourteen stamps issued by the British North American colony of Newfoundland in honor of Queen Victoria's jubilee in the year 1897. This year also marked the four hundredth anniversary of Cabot's voyage. The two events made for a nice philatelic combination. On this historic issue of stamps, Cabot, Henry VII and Cabot's landfall, Cape Bonavista, were all depicted.

This 1497 voyage would take Cabot only nine weeks and would establish England's claim to North America. Cabot's voyage was met with some degree of optimism, but good fortune would abandon him. He and his entire crew were lost during his second voyage. His son, Sebastian Cabot, carried on his work. Eventually the French joined the race for Canada and the rich fur trade. Jacques Cartier established France's claim to North America in his voyage of 1534. The fight for Canada between the English and the French would not be resolved until 1759 with General Wolfe's victory over the French at Quebec. As of 1759, Canada became exclusively England's territory with the exception of two obscure little fishing islands off the coast of Newfoundland called St. Pierre and Miquelon. To this day, the people of those two little islands take their living from the sea in fishing boats as did their ancestors. They also get some income from the sale of the islands' stamps to avid collectors all over the world.

In the pre-1492 exploration period, the ships that dominated European warfare and trade were the cogs. The tubby cogs had a sort of fort or wooden castle at the rear of the ship from which warriors shot arrows and repelled attackers. In time, this part of the ship would be called the sterncastle. The forward part of the cog had a similar structure called the forecastle. This part of the ship became home to the crew. Carricks were more elongated than cogs and had three masts. The first mast, or foremast, carried a square sail. The second mast, or mainmast, carried two square sails arranged one over the other. The last mast, or mizzen mast, carried a triangular or lateen sail. There was also a square sail on the bowsprit at the front of the vessel.

As stated, the French became interested in the exploration of the New World in the early 1500s. Up to this time, only the Spanish and Portuguese had serious interests and the money to fund projects of exploration and colonization. In fact, these two Iberian nations, the most powerful in Europe in 1494, were on the verge of war over the division of the spoils. The problem was resolved by having the pope draw the "Line of Demarcation," which divided the noncolonized world between these two great powers. Spain and Portugal formalized their accord with the pope's line by signing The Treaty of Tordesillas, which gave the world's unclaimed lands to the east of the line to Portugal and those to the west to Spain. On hearing that the pope had divided the New World, Africa and Asia between the Spanish and the Portuguese in the Treaty of Tordesillas, King Francis II of France quipped, "I fail to find that clause in Adam's will."

The French had fine ships of their own. By 1522, Magellan's crew had circumnavigated the world, showing geographers and explorers that the Americas constituted a large land formation that could not be considered anything but a new continent of great mass. Magellan's voyage also proved, beyond the shadow of any doubt, that the earth was round and that the wooden ships of the day could make the heroic voyage of circumnavigation if men could endure some horrible privations like eating rats and boiled boots. This mythic passage would be sought by many over the centuries to come. In 1534, Jacques Cartier sailed to Canada and explored the St. Lawrence River while in search of the Northwest Passage, which he and many other explorers who followed him thought would take them to Japan and China. The great discovery of the time was that the "Lady Without Mercy" had two wild and beautiful sisters that also knew how to torture men and try the strength of their little wooden ships. These siblings of the Atlantic were the Pacific and Indian Oceans.

These oceans had been vaguely known to Europeans and were thought to be all but devoid of islands. After a horrible trip around Cape Horn through the strait that now bears his name, Magellan sailed a few thousand miles from the tip of South America to the Philippines without sighting land. The Philippines proved to be Magellan's undoing. He got involved in a little tribal war between two chiefs and got himself killed for his trouble. His first officer sailed on. By the time his fleet returned to Portugal, it was no longer a fleet. Only one of Magellan's vessels, the *Victoria*, made port after the three-year voyage of circumnavigation. But that one small ship held a huge fortune in spices that paid for the five-ship expedition many times over.

It would be another half-century before any sea captain risked his ship on such a voyage again, and even then, it was because he had no viable alternative. Even Hawaii was not to be discovered until Captain Cook happened on the place in 1778. It is sad to note that the great English explorer was killed by the people of Hawaii over the theft of a ship's boat. In centuries to come, New Englanders would hunt the great whales in all the oceans of the world, and their ships would lead in the China Trade. Hawaii would become a port of call for many a Yankee whaler, but that was still in the future.

The Pacific and Indian Oceans were huge expanses of water that made the Atlantic seem like a very large lake in comparison, only three thousand miles wide. The

Spanish caravels of the fifteenth century.

Atlantic could be crossed in a mere two to three months depending on the weather and the quality of a little ship about a hundred feet in length and 150 tons. A good or bad crossing would also vary on the time of year. The safety of a voyage often depended on pirates from the North African states ruled by thieves who saw piracy as a matter of national economic policy. These Islamic freebooters also ventured into the Atlantic in search of treasure and European slaves. This would remain the case until 1815. The Pacific Ocean was ever so peaceful in its initial appearance that the name "Pacific" was given to it in place of its original appellation, "The Great South Sea," which was bestowed on it by Balboa in 1513 when he crossed the Isthmus of Panama and climbed a tree to get a really good look at it.

The Yankee Fleet

For the most part, early exploration before the Elizabethan Age was left to the richer European nations of Spain, Portugal and France. The English "sea dogs" like Drake, Hawkins, Guy and Gilbert became freelance explorers while in the business of seeking treasure or slaves anywhere and anyway they could. Spain was rich, and England was poor. It was as simple as that. In time, all of the sea dogs turned pirate, in the most respectable sort of way, and took Spain's wealth whenever the opportunity presented itself. In this great enterprise, none was more successful or aggressive than Sir Francis Drake.

He attacked the Spanish directly on the high seas and was bold enough to take his well-armed little ship, the *Golden Hind*, into Spanish ports to seize prizes and treasure on land as well as on the sea. For this reason, after a very successful season of preying on the Spanish settlements and shipping in and around the Atlantic area, and knowing that the Spanish were waiting for him to return to England to ambush him and punish him for his piracy, Drake decided to sail around South America through the Strait of Magellan. Drake surprised everybody by showing up in the Pacific. The Spanish regarded this body of water as their own private preserve, and it had a sort of *de facto* sign on it reading, "Stay Out—Private Property of Their Most Catholic Majesties the King and Queen of Spain."

Drake attacked a Manila galleon, which was all but unarmed. This was a big surprise because there were no ships in the Pacific that would dare to approach the Spanish trading ships under normal circumstances. The Manila galleons were known to carry the whole year's profit from the Spanish Philippines and the rest of the annual Spanish plunder from the Orient to Panama. Here in Central America, the Manila galleon's cargo was to be unloaded and taken over land to the Atlantic Coast to be sent on to the Spanish treasury on a convoy of Spanish ships. For Drake, the Manila galleon was a bonus. Before striking out across the Pacific, Drake had sailed up the California coast and into San Francisco Bay and even went so far as to plant a lead plaque claiming all of California for merry old England and her Queen Elizabeth. Elizabeth was also a major investor in Drake's enterprise and therefore most interested in the outcome of his three-year adventure.

Drake also took on a huge cargo of spices while still in the Pacific and Indian Oceans. He then sailed around the Cape of Good Hope, up the coast of Africa and back home to England after having set out three years before. When Spain's Philip II found out what Drake had been up to, he demanded Drake's head. Queen Elizabeth gave Sir Francis Drake a knighthood instead. She also took her share of the profits. This substantially helped the cash-poor queen to run her country and allowed her to help finance the Dutch who were revolting against Phillip II in the Netherlands. Drake sailed on to many more adventures including a hair-raising little jaunt into the Spanish harbor at Cadiz to burn Philip's navy store of barrel staves. This was both a bold act and a wise move, for without aged wood watertight barrels could not be made. This factor greatly contributed to the defeat of the Spanish Armada in 1588. It seems that most of their water casks leaked because they were made of green wood!

An English shilling of Elizabeth struck about the time Drake was circumnavigating the world.

By 1588, Philip II had become tired of the actions of England and her sea dogs who, in Spain's mind, had become so highhanded that they were no better than common pirates. Elizabeth had refused to punish her pirate friends and had undertaken the unpardonable act of beheading the Catholic heir to Protestant England's throne, Mary Queen of Scots. When the axe fell, Philip II of Spain had his excuse for invading England. With the blessing of the pope, Spain's vast armada of nearly 160 huge galleons sailed against England and her Protestant queen.

England was well championed by her sea dogs in their smaller, sturdier and more maneuverable ships. Drake was under the command of the lord high admiral, the duke of Norfolk. The sea dogs were ready to follow their leaders to hell if asked to. They were hot for battle. Vast piles of wood had been set up all over England in 1588 for bonfires to be lit at the first sight of the Spanish Armada in English home waters. When it showed itself off the Lizard, or Land's End, the fires were lit. When

The Yankee Fleet

Detail from John Smith's map showing English ships of the type used against the Spanish Armada in 1588.

the news came to Drake of the sighting of Philip's fleet, he was playing at bowls. He informed the lord high admiral that he would join him in sailing against the Spanish at the game's conclusion.

Drake's men followed Drake around the world in the years 1577 to 1580, and Queen Elizabeth knighted Drake on the *Golden Hind* at the conclusion of his voyage, after which she received her share of the loot with gratitude. Lacking a large regular navy, the English put together a fleet made up of sea dogs, raiders, armed merchant ships and slavers. The English ships were far smaller than the ships of the Spanish dons. In a close fight, the Spanish tended to fire over them. The English ships were

The Lady Without Mercy

fast and manned by men who understood how to use cannons at a long range. Drake and the duke of Norfolk inspired their men to give their all for Elizabeth and England. The queen had donned a steel breastplate and actually took up her sword, and she joined her men under the command of Lord Dudley. She made a speech to her assembled troops, many of whom were simple farmers who had no experience of war. She addressed her loyal troops saying, "I may not be a king, but I have the heart and the stomach of a king, and a king of England too." They roared and cheered the memory of her father Henry VIII and steeled themselves for the battle that never came. They were happy about that too.

Superior English seamanship, rough seas and the hostile weather all combined to defeat the mighty Spanish Armada. The Spanish dons were chased around the British Isles. Many of the great galleons were wrecked on the northern coasts of Scotland and Ireland where the wild Celts either bashed in the brains of the unfortunate Spanish sailors who fell into their hands or forced them into marriage with their daughters. This is why today one can find Irishmen named Alfonsis O'Sullivan. Of the mighty armada of Philip II, only fifty-eight ships returned to Spain. England's fortunes were on the rise, and her ships were to dominate the oceans of the world for the next 350 years. There were no radical developments in basic form. Eventually, the ships did evolve in size, becoming the classic "East Indiamen" of almost a century later. These bigger ships had three times the tonnage, which allowed them to carry huge cargoes of tea, silk and spices.

The Atlantic is truly a lady without mercy as many a poor seaman could attest, but it is also a beautiful highway that has led to freedom and adventure, both equally seductive.

Chapter 2

THE VOYAGE OF THE *MAYFLOWER* AND HER SISTERS

After the defeat of the Spanish Armada, England was free to exploit the Americas as the Spanish had done for almost a century. One year before the Armada had sailed against England, Sir Walter Raleigh attempted to establish a colony in Virginia. After three years, the settlement disappeared without a trace. In 1607, three small ships made landfall in Virginia. A settlement was founded called Jamestown. This new colony got off to a very shaky start. Nobody seemed to know what he was doing until a draconian little military man by the name of John Smith asserted his authority and bullied the colonists into success. The introduction of tobacco as a cash crop would ensure the success of the colony.

But now comes the great story of triumph over impossible odds. Of course I speak of Plymouth and the all but impossible voyage of the *Mayflower*. To begin with, not everybody on the *Mayflower* held the same religious beliefs as the Pilgrims who called themselves separatists. In fact, the separatists called themselves saints, and those not of their religion were called strangers. The name separatists derived from their desire to separate themselves from the Church of England. John Alden was among the strangers as was Captain Myles Standish, the colony's military leader. As a cooper, or barrel maker, Alden had one of the most important jobs on the *Mayflower*. He was the keeper of the beer. When the passengers could not drink the water because it had turned brackish or had just gone bad because the ship's rats had drowned in it, it was good to know that the beer keeper was on the job.

It is interesting to note that before the voyage there was also a battle raging between two factions of the Pilgrims themselves over the contract between the colonists and the sponsoring investment company that was bankrolling their venture to the New World. Eventually all sides gave in to the company demands. They also gave up a hundred pounds of butter from their provisions to reduce their debts owed to the company. Additionally, the *Mayflower* had originally been charted to arrive at the mouth of the Hudson River, and not in New England as we now define the area. The colonists had also purchased outright the good ship *Speedwell*. The *Speedwell*

The Yankee Fleet

A 1957 cover showing the *Mayflower* carried across the Atlantic by Captain Alan Villiers to Plymouth on the *Mayflower II*.

was smaller than the *Mayflower*, and it was intended that ship would remain with the colonists after the *Mayflower* returned to England. The *Speedwell* was to serve as the new colony's trading vessel, which would be a great advantage as the ship would reduce expenses in the area of shipping fish, lumber, crops and other exports from the colony back to the mother country.

At last in the late summer of 1620, almost too late to set out on a nine- or ten-week voyage across the North Atlantic, the Pilgrims left for their adventure in America. After eight days sailing, the *Mayflower* and the *Speedwell* found themselves beyond the Lizard or Land's End. The *Speedwell's* seams began to open up because its masts were too large, and it carried too much sail. The little ship was under too much strain, and there was nothing to do but return to England. Both ships lumbered back to the place from which they had just sailed. The passengers were removed from the *Speedwell*. After such a rotten start, many of the colonists elected to abandon the voyage and stay in England. The remaining 102 passengers were crowded onto the *Mayflower*, and once again they set out on their voyage hopefully for the last time. Any more false starts might have proved fatal to the success of crossing that year. The Pilgrims had used up far too much precious time already. It was now October, and the North Atlantic was much colder in those days of the mini ice age of the 1600s. The unforgiving Atlantic was not a friendly place for a little 180-ton ship like the *Mayflower*. The one good thing about departing at this late time of year was that the chance of being taken by the Islamic pirates of North Africa was sharply reduced.

The Voyage of the *Mayflower* and Her Sisters

A few weeks out of port, the *Mayflower* ran into bad weather. During the fierce ocean storms that followed, Captain Jones ordered all of the *Mayflower*'s sails reefed. Jones allowed his ship to run before the wind under bare poles. The storms lasted for days, then weeks. The Pilgrims, unused to being at sea, could not keep their food down under such conditions. Not to mention that the food on the voyage was horrible. There was no refrigeration for their perishable supplies, nor was there much variety to their fare even by the standards of the day. Their diet consisted mostly of barley soup, salt beef and stone-solid hardtack that could only be eaten after being soaked in water. The hardtack also housed worms. These hardships were well known to the sailors who took this sort of thing in stride, but these tough experiences were quite foreign to Pilgrims. The colonists could hardly be considered soft by any means, but the hard life that they were accustomed to had been on dry land where they could control their environment to some degree.

To make matters worse, the principal structural beam, which supported the mainmast, cracked, causing the integrity of the footing of the mainmast itself to be compromised. This meant that no sails could be set on the mainmast, and no strain could be allowed on the main beam. The *Mayflower* was at risk of becoming a floating coffin adrift on the unforgiving Atlantic. Given enough time on the high seas without food, and travelers becoming more desperate, even cannibalism might not have been unthinkable as the ship aimlessly drifted. But John Alden remembered the house jack that had been purchased for the lifting of heavy beams in the construction of buildings in the new colony, and he suggested that it be used to brace the cracked beam. The screw was put into place and turned. The cracked beam drew together and closed. Sails could now be set on the mainmast again, and the ship and the voyage were saved. Captain Jones grunted his thanks and nodded his head, showing his appreciation to Alden for resolving the problem.

Now the Pilgrims could get back to the cold comfort of the awful food and miserable conditions of life aboard the ship. It might be considered a mercy that the water was undrinkable because there was such an attractive alternative. Beer was consumed in place of the brackish water to the measurable amount of one gallon a day for every man, woman and child aboard the ship. Since a small child could not drink a gallon of beer in the course of a day, we can assume that some people were drinking more than their share. Now that would have made this rotten voyage more tolerable.

The sailors aboard the *Mayflower* had no sympathy for their hapless passengers, and they treated them with contempt and made sport of tormenting them. The sailors made fun of the Pilgrims and their unconventional beliefs without any admonishment from Captain Jones. The major source of contempt was the fact that most of the Pilgrims were seasick a good deal of the time. William Bradford, who would become Plymouth's second governor after the death of John Carver in 1621, reports in his journal that one old salt was a great deal more abusive than the rest of the crew. His poetic fate would be discussed later by Bradford in his journal with some relish.

The Yankee Fleet

A ship of the Pilgrim period from an old print.

The Voyage of the *Mayflower* and Her Sisters

None of the professional sailors on the *Mayflower* was too pleased with the late fall voyage to America to begin with. The North Atlantic is at its most unforgiving at that time of the year. Even the most seasoned old tar hated sailing in late fall. The sailors blamed the troublesome colonists for their general state of constant discomfort. They were sick to death over the separatists' constant squabbling with the voyage's backers, which had delayed the sailing date so late into the season. Like many fundamentalist sects, the Pilgrims were strangers to the art of diplomacy and compromising. This had been very true even when they were rendering judgment on their neighbors back in England. They accused nonseparatists of being too Roman or even pagan. They also accused the Church of England of being both papist and pagan at the same time, which was a neat trick no matter how you look at it. The Pilgrims had stripped away all traces of the Catholic faith in their unvarnished theology and meetinghouses. Unlike the Church of England, which had retained many trappings of the old Roman Catholic Church, such as the use of vestments, altar cloths and candles, as well as the form of the Mass itself, the separatists had abandoned such "Roman trash." A tolerant sect they were not.

James I, king of England, Scotland and Ireland, son of Mary Queen of Scots and chief promoter of the *King James Bible*, newly translated under his own instructions, was not at all pleased to be called names by this ragtag crowd of religious nonconformists from Scrooby. James was not amused at all, and cried, "Do they call me a Pagan? Bring them before me, and I shall deal with them!"

Elder Brewster and the other offending separatists were hauled before the king who was a true intellectual and Renaissance prince. King James I questioned them on complex issues of theology, and he totally confounded them. Then he dressed them down for their presumptuous and inflammatory statements directed against the Church of England of which he was the undisputed head. King James's wrath was terrible, and the separatists were frightened out of their wits by the intensity of his royal fury. James had written a number of books including an antismoking bestseller entitled *A Counterblast to Tobacco*. In this work, the king declared that the weed destroyed the health of his subjects, undermined their character, made them lazy and made chimneys of their noses. He was more than 350 years ahead of his time in his condemnation of the "sot weed" as tobacco was often called. Even more, he did this in the face of the fact that tobacco was a huge part of his income from the plantations of Virginia. James made the point crystal clear that he would not endure insults of a religious nature from a bunch of lower middle class farmers and artisans who thought themselves morally superior to him and his church.

The sailors, no doubt, found the Pilgrims to be just as disagreeable as the king did and as the citizens of Scrooby did, the Pilgrim's own hometown. The Pilgrims had fought their fellow citizens who were members of the Church of England. They also fought each other in the streets during their self-imposed exile in the Netherlands before they returned to England and elected to try their luck in America. People who style themselves "saints" make difficult neighbors. And now they were on the high seas amongst sailors who hated their self-righteous attitudes They were also hungry, dirty, overcrowded, cold, often wet, sickened by the tossing of the little ship and even scorned by the captain himself. Captain Jones could only think of making landfall and then heading back to England after dumping off his sorry burden of passengers. Bradford recorded in his journal the trials and tribulations of the unhappy colonists during the voyage, but he also recorded with some satisfaction that the sailor bully, mentioned before, who had been the chief tormentor of the Pilgrims had died and was sewn in his hammock and then dropped into the Atlantic without much ceremony. I am very sure that the Pilgrims thought that it was the judgment of God upon him for his tormenting of God's anointed people. After all, they had deemed themselves saints.

After a passage of nine weeks, land was sighted to the relief of all. Given the season, the voyage had been horrible. Bartholomew Gosnold had named the bit of land off which the Pilgrims now found themselves Cape Cod because his ship "had been so pestered with ye cod that we could barely move." The sailors would have been quite content to drop their passengers on the beach or into the surf and then beat it back across the wild Atlantic even though it was now December and the Atlantic was at its most ferocious. However, Jones dropped anchor, and Captain Standish and a party of well-armed men began to explore the region for the purpose of locating a settlement. After looking about a bit, the Pilgrims boarded their boat or pinnace to sail along the shoreline. They landed on Cape Cod and discovered some stores of grain corn. This they took, declaring it to be a gift from God. They also opened some Indian graves and took some of the grave goods. The natives that they encountered ran away, but at one point there was a skirmish. The word was spreading among the indigenous population across the Cape that there were strange looking men running about with loud weapons and wearing odd clothing who were stealing food and breaking into graves. As a result, the Pilgrims did not feel welcome or safe on the Cape, and they were forced to make sail for a more friendly shore where they had not violated anybody's sensibilities.

Captain Jones had attempted to go to the agreed destination of the Pilgrim settlement, which was to be the mouth of the Hudson River—discovered a dozen years before by Henry Hudson—but the currents were running far too strong and prevented such a landing. Captain Jones then sailed to the northwest of Cape Cod Bay and told the Pilgrims to find a place quickly, or he would leave them on the beach at a place of his own choosing. The Pilgrims loudly complained that this treatment was inhumane, but the captain and his sailors had been determined to attempt a return home in the *Mayflower* before the weather got any worse. However, it was now December, when the North Atlantic was at its most terrible, and it became obvious that the *Mayflower* would have to winter off the New England coast. This ugly fact didn't make the sailors love the Pilgrims any more.

The December temperatures were now well below freezing. The men who continued to go out in the small boat were soaked to the waist most of the time.

The Voyage of the *Mayflower* and Her Sisters

A map of Cape Cod and the islands from Samuel Adams Drake's book, *Nooks and Corners of the New England Coast*, published in 1875.

They did a great deal of wading in the water in their search for a place to settle. All of them caught pneumonia. William Bradford himself fell profoundly ill and almost died. It was fortunate for all of the settlers that he recovered and lived to govern the colony from 1621 to 1657. He alone had the strength to hold the Plymouth Colony together in the years ahead. He was a rational man who was able to reconcile the various factions within the settlement. He authored a fantastic historic account of the colony in his journal that covered more than a quarter-century of its life. This remarkable journal was lost and found, then lost and found again, but that's another story. Bradford was, in addition to everything else, a leading contributor to the first governing document of Plymouth Colony, the Mayflower Compact. This agreement was signed by the forty-one adult males who made up the colony. And the rest is history. Plymouth was to be the first successful English settlement in New England.

Because the *Mayflower* didn't sink and join countless other vessels, powered by sail, at the bottom of the cold waters of the Atlantic, the epic voyage of the *Mayflower* and the settlement of Plymouth Colony represent a great American saga that has evolved over the years. The savage Atlantic yielded up life for the Pilgrims in the form of fish and lobsters, but it also produced a harvest of death. In 1635, the worst hurricane in recorded history up until the disastrous Long Island Express in the late summer of 1938 struck New England. William Bradford in Plymouth and John Winthrop in Boston each recorded the story of the monumental storm in their respective journals. Bradford wrote, "Such a mighty storm of wind and rain as none having in these parts, either English or Indian, ever saw…It blew down sundry houses and uncovered others [ripped the roofs off the structures]…It blew down many hundreds of thousands of trees, turning up the stronger by the roots and breaking the higher pine trees off in the middle."

The winds whipped about the sea and shore for five days before the awful storm actually struck in August of 1635. When it struck in its full fury, its winds were estimated at 130 miles per hour. A huge storm surge ran up onto the shore about twenty-one feet in height at Buzzard's Bay and fourteen feet high at the more sheltered port of Providence, Rhode Island. Massachusetts Bay Colony's governor, John Winthrop, wrote in his journal on August 16, 1635, "It blew with such violence, with an abundance of rain, that it blew down many hundreds of trees, overthrew some houses and drove ships from their anchors. Eight of ye Indians were sucked under the waters while flying from their wigwams."

During such storms, ships may have been much safer with sails reefed and facing into the storm, far out at sea where they were safe from rocks and the hostile shoreline. The Atlantic could toss a ship about while at sea, and the vessel could ride it out safely under bare poles as the *Mayflower* had done in 1620. Should a sailing ship be tossed on the rocks or on the shore itself, its hull would be cracked like a walnut. Many a fine sailing vessel left its bones bleaching in the sun on the Cape's shores. On one sunny afternoon, Henry David Thoreau lunched on one such skeleton, the victim of the Atlantic's gentle mercies, during his walking trip along the shores of Cape Cod.

The rest of Plymouth's story is well-known history. As stated, Plymouth would be the first successful settlement in New England. As the late and great historian, author and dean of social science at Massachusetts's Bridgewater State College, Dr. Jordan D. Fiore, once remarked, "Plymouth looms so largely in American History because it is such a great story of human survival against all odds. It is essentially just that—a good story."

But before the *Mayflower*, there were three little ships that had carried settlers to Jamestown in Virginia in 1607. The story of this colony is also a story of struggle

Captain John Smith as depicted on a map from his book *The Generall Historie of Virginia, New England, and the Summer Isle*, published in 1624.

against the elements both of nature and of man. There were a number of significant ships in Virginia's history whose voyages shaped life in that colony. In 1619, a Dutch sailing ship brought slaves to Jamestown. This practice of slavery would grow to poison the nation that was to evolve out of Britain's thirteen colonies. Slavery was a nearly fatal affliction that has only now really begun to heal some four centuries later.

Also in 1619, there came from England a ship filled with "ninety maids of virtue." This ship was referred to as the wife ship. This vessel landed the scarcest commodity in Jamestown, namely women. I have often wondered that the directors of the Virginia Company never considered the fact that women were essential to the growth and success of any civilization. The founders of the Virginia Company were living in a very lusty age. I can't help but question how this obvious fact seemed to escape their notice. This was not the Victorian Era when the function of sex in society was hidden as something so vulgar as to be beyond the notice of middle-class people. Why did they only send men to colonize Virginia in 1607? I guess they were just too preoccupied by dreams of riches.

Jamestown was basically an all male affair in its first dozen years. This would suggest that there wasn't much Anglo population growth in the colony. Jamestown exported a fortune in sot weed, or tobacco, to England where it sold very well. In Jamestown, it was even grown in the streets according to popular stories. The Virginia Company wanted to ensure the future of their tobacco empire in America, which had turned out to be a gold mine, hence the providing of women to those poor, lonesome male colonists. Officers of the company sought women suitable for their program of settlement in England's prisons. It was explained to the women that a respectable marriage in Jamestown was better than life in England's hellholes for stealing, streetwalking or murder.

The willing brides were auctioned off upon their arrival in Jamestown to their husbands. Payment was made in hogsheads of tobacco. Many an aristocratic Old Dominion family has a few ancestors who came to America almost four hundred years ago on the wife ship. Other ships also followed with more fallen women who were transformed into paragons of virtue by an ocean voyage. In a very tangible way the sea provided for just about everything including practical romance. The end result was that the future of Virginia was assured.

Some of the ships crossing the Atlantic from England were only forty feet in length. Many a man had dreamed of walking the narrow deck of a little ship on a voyage to America. Such was the case in 1607 when a decision was made to colonize northern Virginia and establish the Popham Colony. The Popham Colony never had the chance to become as well grounded as Jamestown. It was located in what is today Maine, which was an extremely cold place during the mini ice age of the period. Few Englishmen had ever experienced anything like winter in Maine. Even today, with the earth warming, winter in Maine is still very cold.

But in the year 1607, at the height of summer, things in Maine seemed fine. The colonists had a fair crossing as the Atlantic is on her best behavior at that time of the year. The Pophamites built a settlement that they called Fort George in honor of their patron, George Popham, the founder of the colony. They developed many projects including a new enterprise, namely shipbuilding. Axes rang out their song of labor as trees were felled in the Maine forests. The Popham Colony had fine stands of tall pine that were tight ringed and old. Both tall and straight, those trees yielded fine wide boards, timbers and masts. During an archaeological dig in 1999, a caulking iron, found in what must have been a colonial Popham storehouse almost four hundred years old, gave mute evidence of the shipbuilding activity on the shores of the Kennebec. Two centuries later, shipbuilding would become a well-established fact of commercial life in Maine. It seems that 1608 was just not the right time for such a venture. But the little Maine-built ship *Virginia* showed that it could be done.

Four centuries ago, saw pits yielded up hand-sawed boards, and a little ship was framed. From the facts that I can gather together, it must have been a one-masted vessel of something less than forty feet in length. It was fully decked and could carry a considerable amount of cargo; this little vessel was named the *Virginia* after the colony that claimed rule over this settlement.

The *Virginia* was the first ship built in British America. It made at least two ocean voyages. One of these ocean trips was to Jamestown. The winter of 1607–1608 was a very hard one, and the colonists suffered a great deal from the icy cold and hostile climate. Spring came and then passed into summer as 1608 wore on. By the time fall rolled around, the population of the colony had lost all ambition to nurture the northern part of Virginia into a blooming civilization. The colonists packed up their goods and sailed back to England, which was looking very comfortable and welcoming indeed. The *Virginia* was not to be the last ship built in Maine or New England. In its way, that little fully decked ship launched the proud history of the age of sail, which would reach well into the twentieth century. It all began on the shores of the Kennebec with the construction and launching of the little *Virginia*.

More and more sailing ships would bring colonists to the shores of New England. In 1630, a huge fleet, which included the *Mayflower*, brought thousands of colonists to the Massachusetts Bay Colony. This well-heeled group of settlers was of the Puritan religion. They established a theocratic state under the governorship of John Winthrop in their capital city of Boston. Winthrop meant it to be "a shining city on a hill," an example to all the world of what Godly perfection on earth could be like. Boston had a fine harbor, and Atlantic shipping in and out of this well-protected harbor began almost at once. Boston prospered by the sea and was deemed by its inhabitants "The Athens of the New World" and "The Hub of the Universe." They may have lacked a certain modesty, but Bostonians certainly had style.

New Hampshire was also settled in the 1620s. The port of Portsmouth became a most important shipping center vital to the new colony. Sir Ferdinando Gorges became New Hampshire's principal leader. He was willing to join Massachusetts in common defense, but Massachusetts Governor John Winthrop was not willing to do that. He even wrote in his journal, "Those of Sir Fernando George his province

The landing of the Pilgrims from a nineteenth-century print.

beyond the Piscourse from us, both in their ministry and civil administration; for they had lately made Accomenticus [a poor village] a corporation, and had made a taylor [sic] their mayor, and had entertained a [Rev.] Mr. Hull, an excommunicated person, and a very contentious minister."

As we can see, New Hampshireites were almost as objectionable as Rhode Islanders were to the Puritans of Massachusetts Bay Colony. Roger Williams had been thrown out of Massachusetts in 1635. He was viewed as a bad seed hopelessly infected with the delusion of religious toleration. By 1636, Williams had founded the new colony of Rhode Island and Providence Plantations, and he threw the doors open to anybody who wanted to move there regardless of their religion. Williams supported the "strange" idea that anyone should be able to worship as they pleased including Catholics, Jews and people of no religious convictions whatsoever. Williams could never be forgiven by the intolerant Massachusetts theocracy for that heresy.

Newport, Rhode Island, became one of the truly great colonial commercial ports. It was of such importance that Fort Adams would be constructed here over a century and a half later to protect it during the War of 1812. During the Revolution, Count D'Estaing and the French fleet harbored here. It was also a great summer resort

The Voyage of the *Mayflower* and Her Sisters

Dreams of discovering the Northwest Passage were never given up even as late as 1874 as seen here in this cartoon of Benjamin Disraeli. From *Punch*, "Dreaming of its Discovery 265 Years After Henry Hudson's Fatal Attempt."

town enjoyed by the West Indies planters in the eighteenth century. New York society also enjoyed the place as a watering hole long after the port passed into commercial oblivion. Today the International Tennis Hall of Fame is located here. Great mansions of the early republic blend with the palatial houses built by the eighteenth-century merchant class whose great fortunes in some way came from the sea. Here the American castles of the belle epoque can still be seen and visited. The houses all rub aristocratic shoulders with each other in a strange architectural harmony.

The folks who built these fine mansions may have been looked down upon by Boston Brahmins and Main Line Philadelphia society, but the Newport summer visitors had the cash to buy the aristocratic titles of many an ancient European royal or aristocratic family hard up for funds. Even the ducal house of Marlborough, the family of the noble Churchills, dipped into the great American genetic well of

The Yankee Fleet

commercial success when a future duke of Marlborough married a daughter of the Vanderbilts. Surely her five million dollars helped seal the deal. However, the bride was not happy, and she later left the short duke with bad breath and bad teeth, but not before she fixed up the ancestral digs and produced "the heir and the spare" as she styled the duke's two sons by her.

Connecticut was founded about the same time as Rhode Island. It was another Puritan theocracy where the Bible and its strictures were the law. It also owed its wealth to the sea and the trade carried on by ships. New London and other port cities welcomed merchantmen and whale men alike. You can still go to Mystic and see the last surviving whaler of its generation, the *Charles W. Morgan*, at anchor looking much as it did in the 1840s when it sailed the Atlantic, Pacific and Indian Oceans in the business of catching, cutting into and trying down the whale for its oil.

The *Mayflower*, and all the thousands of other vessels that sailed to these American shores, played a role in developing a nation that would owe its life to wooden ships and the ironmen who went to sea and served under the crisp snap of sail. The relationship between the Atlantic and the colonists was at best a grossly uneven contest between mere mortals and the mighty ocean. But the romance enjoyed with this hard and salty deep is a story of true lovers' total devotion to each other in a most tempestuous relationship. And in the end, one must conclude that Massachusetts owes its life to the beautiful Atlantic and the treasure it holds.

Chapter 3

A Rover's Life

Now, as a child, who didn't dream of being a pirate? I think most little boys play at being pirates at some time in their lives, and maybe a few girls aspire to be female pirates like Mary Read or Anne Bonny. This is most true when one lives not too far from the sea. By 1733, all thirteen original British colonies had been established along the Atlantic Coast from the District of Maine in the north to Georgia in the south. All of these entities had some brushes with buccaneers. The District of Maine, where so many fine schooners were to be built, was actually part of Massachusetts Bay and would remain so until Henry Clay hammered out the Missouri Compromise in 1820. Maine became an independent state of the federal union because of Clay's efforts to head off a civil war between the free and slave states. Maine's becoming a free state was balanced by Missouri becoming a slave state, thus preserving the balance of power between the free states and the slave states in the United States Senate.

New England owed its life to the Atlantic and the intrinsic treasure it held. The codfish itself was not the least of these. In point of fact, the Sacred Cod, carved of pine and lovingly painted over two centuries ago, still hangs in the Massachusetts Statehouse designed by Bullfinch. This piscatorial tribute paid by The Great and General Court of the Commonwealth of Massachusetts is a true homage to the great Atlantic, which breathed life into the state situated on the bay.

The riches of Massachusetts, New Hampshire, Rhode Island and Connecticut were shipped out of Boston, Salem, Newport and the ports of Connecticut, Mystic and New London, which were to see the rise and fall of the whaling fishery and all the wealth it brought to the Nutmeg State. All of this wealth eventually lured a whole tribe of freebooters who would go sailing "on account" as piracy was styled. Many a lad harbored romantic notions of the roving life of a pirate. These youngsters never really thought about the bad food, sadistic pirate captains, dangers of life on the high seas or of falling into the hands of a more powerful pirate or the king's navy. Nor did they consider that they might become one of those sun-dried, mummified corpses hung in chains as a cadaverous warning to all pirates, and would-be pirates, of the full vigor, scope and measure of the king's justice.

The first pirate to sail New England waters was Dixey Bull. He came to Boston from London in 1631, the first year after the city's founding. He bought a small vessel and engaged in trade with the towns along the coast of the District of Maine, which was part of Plymouth Colony. In Penobscot Bay he was attacked by an armed party of Frenchmen in a small boat. Dixey wasn't pleased with this event, and he made a conscious choice to turn to piracy. He travelled back down to Boston and picked up a crew of young bloods who were willing to try something other than farming to make a living in this new country. Captain Dixey Bull then made quite a name for himself in the pirating trade, attacking not only French shipping but English shipping as well. Once asked why he went after the ships of his own countrymen even in preference to the French, he replied that the English had more money and richer cargoes.

His ambitions knew no bounds, and he decided to attack fortified towns as well as cargo ships. Dixey sailed boldly into Pemaquid Harbor with a flotilla of three ships. He bombarded the fort with his cannons and took the town. The citizens fled into the woods, and Dixey sacked the town, taking everything of value. It is said that like all good pirates he buried his treasure. But like many pirates, he never returned to enjoy it. So, where is Dixey's loot today? It is rumored to be stashed on Damariscove Island and on Cushing Island in Casco Bay. As to what happened to Dixey Bull, nobody seems to know for sure, but there are rumors that he angered a fisherman by the name of Daniel Curtis who called him out. A duel followed on an island not far off the coast from Pemaquid where the enraged colonist killed him. There are also rumors that the Royal Navy caught up with him and that Dixey was returned to London for trial and was judged guilty and hanged at Tyburn.

The last pirate hanged in Boston in the good old Commonwealth of Massachusetts was a son of sunny Spain, Francisco Ruiz. Ruiz took up the pirating trade in the 1830s, long after many thought that its day had passed. My thoughts are that he just wasn't very good at it, and he tended to leave a good many witnesses alive to tell the tail of his depredations, which is never a good thing for an ambitious pirate to do. At the time of his capture, there were a great number of victims all alive and willing to give evidence against him. Pirates were not loved any more in 1835, when Ruiz went to trial, than they were in 1631. As a result, Ruiz was found guilty, and he enjoyed the distinct honor of being the last man hanged for piracy in Boston.

Between 1631 and 1835, there were a lot of other freebooters willing to take prizes up and down the Atlantic Coast. Ships from Philadelphia, the largest and richest commercial colonial center, and the rich trading vessels passing in and out of the harbor of New York were also sure to receive the attention of pirates. Philadelphia and other growing cities along the coast of British America sent out rich cargoes and received them as well. England also traded with the Carolinas, Georgia, Virginia, New England and the middle colonies. Charleston's port was very attractive to the pirate confraternity. In the heyday of piracy, between the mid-1600s and the first

Anne Bonny's image on a box carved about 1780.

third of the 1700s, thousands of fat prizes valued at millions of pounds of sterling were on their way to and from the English colonies on the waves of the wide Atlantic. And many lusty lads, along with a couple of lusty girls, like the aforementioned Mary Read and Anne Bonny, who sailed with Calico Jack Rackham, were anxious to go on account and make their fortune.

Piracy is as old as the act of shipping goods over the water. The Romans knew pirates well, and how to deal with them. As a youth, Julius Caesar was captured by pirates and held for ransom. The plucky teenager warned his captors that he meant to return after his ransom was paid and punish the pirates for the treatment he had suffered. They laughed at his youthful bragging. He was eventually ransomed, freed and sent back to Rome where he organized his scheme of revenge. He returned to the pirates' lair to exact an awful price of his own for his humiliation. Payback is good. "Thus be it ever to pirates," was the sentiment of old Europe.

In the Middle Ages, the Vikings attacked Rome and Constantinople. One Viking chief went so far in his piratical enthusiasm as to carve his name in the altar rail of Santa Sophia Catholic Church during his raid on the mighty Byzantine imperial capital of Constantinople. Even monks went on account, preying on the trade of the northern European commercial cities that were dominated by the wealthy rising middle class of professional merchants. In the face of the savage attacks on their trade and the depredations of the pirates on free cities like Danzig, Hamburg, Bremen and others, these rising commercial centers united to form the Hansa to deal with this economic threat. The Hanseatic League was dedicated to the extermination of pirates. Their ships—high-sterned cogs with tall, well-fortified sterncastles and forecastles— swept the seas of freebooters, religious (a few former monks) or otherwise.

It was only a short time before piracy made its way to the rich American world of commerce. Not long after the Spanish began to exploit the riches of the New World, a class of buccaneers emerged to steal treasure from the Spanish dons on the high seas. This was because only the Spanish had anything worth stealing during the better part of the sixteenth century. Most of these freebooters were English or French with a few Dutchmen tossed in for good measure. The French had been slaughtering cattle in the West Indies for some time, so they observed how easy it would be to take it one step further, slaughtering men and taking the Spanish treasure galleons on the high seas.

Switching from the cattle trade to piracy is what we would today call a career change or a lateral move. The name given to the French butchers, "buccaneers," was used to designate their new profession of piracy. There were some great monsters among these early freebooters. One of the earliest writers to celebrate these career criminals was John Esquemeling, a colonial doctor who had even treated Henry Morgan himself. His definitive work, *The Buccaneers of America: A True Account of the Most Remarkable Assaults Committed of Late Years Upon the Coasts of the West Indies*

Sir Henry Morgan, "Our English Jamaican Hero," as depicted in an old copperplate engraving from Esquemeling's *The Buccaneers of America*.

by the Buccaneers of Jamaica and Tortuga (Both English and French) Wherein are Contained More Especially the Unparalleled Exploits of Sir Henry Morgan, our English Jamaican Hero, Who Sacked Porto Bello, Burnt Panama, etc., became popular reading. One of the very first, or maybe the first, edition of Esquemeling's book was most likely printed in Amsterdam in 1678. It was printed in London in 1684 and 1685 and was a runaway bestseller all over Europe and in America as well. If you are wondering how a pirate like Henry Morgan came to be called a hero, you have to understand the political dynamics of Europe at the time. There was a great conflict between Catholic and Protestant nations at the time, but trade and nationalistic ambitions were still the chief motivating factor in these international rivalries.

After all, the Protestant pirate Morgan did some pretty horrible things to his Spanish Catholic victims. When he attacked some of the settlements in Spanish America, he often faced some bad odds as he was frequently outnumbered. To shorten the odds a bit, Morgan once seized a convent full of nuns and a monastery filled with monks. He marched these religious folks out in front of his men to shield them from the fire of the Spanish troops. In Europe, religion and politics were historically joined at the hip. The religion of the king was the religion of the land, and one's religious affiliation was a matter of patriotism. But regardless of one's own religious prejudices, marching unarmed women and men in front of your ranks is beyond the pale even if their faith seems rather unusual.

The Spanish, being very religious, were in an ethical and moral fix. They were taking the English pirates' fire and knew that they could not return fire without killing the nuns and monks who were being used as human shields by Morgan. In the end, the Spanish had no choice but to defend themselves. Many of the monks and nuns died in the crossfire, and the Spanish forces lost to the pirates anyway because they deliberated too long while Morgan's men were picking them off. As Protestant Englishmen, loyal and true, it was probably easy for the men to justify the slaughter as they saw the Spanish Catholic faith as a source of repression. In the end, the event was motivated by nationalistic and political standings with just a bit of bigotry tossed in for good measure. It is interesting to note that Henry Morgan was knighted by King Charles II for his "good work" against the Spanish in the Americas. As an added bonus, Morgan was made lieutenant governor of Jamaica and given the job of hunting down pirates. In his fifties, all of the excesses of his old life caught up with him, and wracked with pain he died a prematurely old man. But not even his grave site was spared by the same forces of nature that rule the wide and deep Atlantic that had been Morgan's home and the scene of his calling. During an earthquake, his grave, body and monument all fell into the sea and were lost forever. This was a fitting end to Sir Henry Morgan. It was indeed poetic justice. Sic transit gloria mundi et gloria Morgani.

Port Royal, the great center of pirating, was also dumped into the ocean by an earthquake as the ultimate disapproval of nature to such an unnatural sink of corruption. Esquemeling's book was equally as popular as Cotton Mather's work on

Morgan's men sack Puerto del Principe. From Esquemeling's *The Buccaneers of America*.

witchcraft in America, which was also a contemporary bestseller. The Esquemeling book was even published in Spain in 1682 and 1684. Everybody who could read wanted to know all about pirates' lives just like we want to know all about the intimate details of strange celebrities' lives today. And like contemporary taste, the more sordid the book, the better. It's like some bizarre situations back in the 1400s when hundreds or even thousands of people would attend an execution and loudly cry out in sympathy for the condemned. But if a last minute reprieve should arrive, the people observing the unhappy event would then go into a collective rage because they were being denied their promised savage amusement. Saddened and even shocked by this horrible feeling of being cheated, they would work themselves into a frenzy and then rip the reprieved man limb from limb.

When Morgan himself read Esquemeling's book, he was horrified. Esquemeling had been Morgan's doctor and knew far too much about him. The book was too accurate for the former pirate's taste. Now that he wanted to be respectable, Morgan could not have the English world reading about his wretched behavior. He sued and won cases against the English publishers in the amount of twenty thousand pounds. Exposing pirates is an expensive business even if you are telling the truth. Morgan was very interested in his place in history, and it must have saddened him in the end that he would never be truly respectable even though he had broken bread with King Charles II and had gained a knighthood. Esquemeling's book is still read today, airing Morgan's dirty laundry for the entertainment of others.

The first of the post–sea dogs, the second generation of true pirates, did not have big ships as a rule. At first, the French and English freebooters, buccaneers, men on account, rovers or pirates had small craft. For the most part, they attacked their prey, both rich and not so rich, at night in these little boats close to the American shores. They boarded the anchored ships and attacked the unsuspecting crews by stealth. Then they would loot the vessels and return to their base. They would live it up until the money was gone, and then they would set out again on another pirating adventure to once more fill their purse. In the beginning, it was a sort of shore cottage industry or part-time job for these adventuresome fellows. Eventually the law of averages would catch up with most of them, and the game would be up. They would be tried, found guilty and executed. Their lifeless corpses would dangle twisting in the wind on gibbets, between the low tide and the high tide, until the seabirds and sea life had cleaned their bones of flesh. For those who specialized in piracy, on this bush league level life was not long or very rewarding. Either a quick death in battle or a lingering death from wounds after the battle or a nasty death at the end of a rope or a messy death at the blade of an axe man was most often their fate after a career of less than a few years duration. One thing is for sure. A pirate's life was not a happy one and totally lacked real glamour.

But alas, it was a short step from capturing a ship to making it one's own true pirate vessel. A lucky pirate could capture a better ship than the one he had and trade up or even build a pirate fleet. Pirates themselves were sort of free spirits to whom following orders was intolerable. For the most part, pirate society was the most democratic in the world. Pirates elected their own captains and officers, with few exceptions, on the basis of their abilities to lead and fight, as well as navigate and bring success to their enterprises. I suppose that getting elected captain could also involve an intimidation factor as in the case of the gigantic Blackbeard. At his great height of between six feet, two inches and six feet, six inches, he could command the respect of his would-be followers without too much trouble. He overawed his men into giving him unconditional support and total control over their lives. This isn't too hard to understand when one considers that Blackbeard was a giant by any standard given that the average seventeenth-century Anglo-American was about five feet, two inches tall and weighed on average 115 pounds.

Blackbeard's manner of control (or leadership style as we would say today) was far from conventional. He would force his men into drinking contests to the point that they all passed into a state of total alcoholic insensibility. Most of his men became very ill, or just died. Sometimes, just for a change of pace, Blackbeard would engage in another type of contest of human endurance. One fine summer day in the subtropics, he led his men below decks and closed all the hatches. He then had his men drain a few bumpers of rum. "No hardship yet," was what most of them must have thought even in the horrible heat. But at this juncture, the game changed. Blackbeard put out the candles and lit some slow-burning matches that had been braided into his beard. This wreathed his face in a weird unearthly light. Laughing loudly, he then lit several bowls of sulfur on fire to light up his little party in the sealed and very hot space below decks. The men cried, screamed, cursed and pleaded between pathetic whimpers, quite unbecoming for members of the pirate brotherhood, to be let out of Blackbeard's inferno. He just roared peals of demonic laughter at them. Hellishly loud peals of laughter there were too, until the first man died. At that point, he opened the hatches and allowed those who could to crawl out onto the deck where he strode about them and laughed them to scorn while kicking a few here and there just to prove the point that he was the far better man and captain beyond all shadow of doubt.

Once in a while, when a substantial portion of his men were gathered in the great common cabin, this fun-loving sociopath would put a grin on his face and place his hands under the table. Some of the crew would take notice of this strange behavior and of the devilishly delighted look on Blackbeard's smiling face. Anybody who knew that look would make every effort to quietly slip away from the impending proceedings unobserved. All of a sudden, two successive explosions would go off, and two unfortunate members of the crew would fall to the deck grabbing shattered legs. What the captain had done was to take a pair of pistols in his hands, and while his hands were under the table, he would wait until he was unobserved. He would then fire his weapons just to see what would happen. Such was his intellectual curiosity. I find it interesting to speculate just what little five-year-old Blackbeard must have been like growing up in England before he went to sea and sailed off into

BLACKBEARD, THE PIRATE.

Very early engraving of the pirate Blackbeard.

a pirate's life in America. First of all, his real name was Edward Teach, and he went off to sea as a commercial sailor when very young. He later fell in with pirates and adopted that way of life as his own, finding it a much more exciting alternative than his previous lifestyle.

In his own way, I suppose that he cared for his men. Every sailing ship in those days had a medicine chest provided for the care of the crew. The folk medicine practiced by the pirates was most likely of a better standard than that practiced by the unlearned quacks on shore. For pirates learned the medical arts by trial and error and constant practice due to the nature of their chosen calling. When the medicine chest ran low on the expensive nostrums, the pirates would get a bit anxious. To show that he was on top of the situation, Blackbeard blockaded the port of Charleston, South Carolina, and seized several of the town's most outstanding citizens, not to mention some very pretty ones. He then informed the governor of the Carolinas and the government of the town that the blockade would not be lifted, or the hostages returned, until a chest of medicines was delivered to his ship.

The good citizens of Charleston, knowing Blackbeard well, complied with his wishes and delivered up the chest as requested. Blackbeard released his hostages and sailed away. It must have pained him to give up all his hostages, especially the pretty ones, as he had an eye for the ladies and even contemplated marriage with the daughter of an important colonial official. When one stops to think of it, under the right circumstances, he might have been a good catch. He was a good provider with a steady income, and by the standards of the day, he was as upright a fellow as say, Sir Henry Morgan. There may even have been a king's pardon in the works. He was on a friendly basis with more than a few colonial officials. However, society probably wouldn't have reacted too kindly to the introduction: "I'd like you to meet my son-in-law the pirate!"

One of the earliest stories ever told to me about Blackbeard was related by my Aunt Charlotte when I was about six years old. According to her, Blackbeard liked the ladies a lot. In fact, it was rumored that he had actually married quite a number of them. Like a lot of romantics, Blackbeard could fall out of love as quickly as he had fallen into it. When the bloom was off the marital rose, he would turn to his bride of the moment and say, "Would ye like to see me treasure me dear?" His wife would get all excited and reply, "Oh yes! Please," no doubt thinking, "Here's the big payoff."

Indeed it was the big payoff. According to my aunt, Blackbeard would lead his bride to a cave deep inside a hill until he reached a door of thick oak that had huge iron hinges and was triple bolted and secured by three huge steel locks. His wife would be beside herself with anticipation of the treasure to come. Blackbeard would then unbolt the door and unlock the three huge locks. He would light a torch from the one he carried, and say to his bride, "Ye may enter me dear, and whatsoever ye may be able to carry off shall be yours."

Blackbeard most likely smiled kindly, and his eyes might have even fluttered a bit with true benevolence as his wife rushed in to claim her treasure. She would squeal with delight as she saw jewels of unsurpassed beauty and cloth of gold. Then she would see piles of silver and gold bullion and bolts of silk, but then she would see something else quite disturbing. On closer inspection of Blackbeard's cave, there appeared skeletons of women still dressed in their finery. She would then hear the door slamming into place behind her and the bolts being slid into their locked positions, and then the keys themselves being turned in the locks. The last sound would be Blackbeard's voice saying, "Ye may have all ye can carry away me darling."

Is it true? Who knows. Who cares. It makes a good story and tells more about the man than any dry history. I was told that there may be more of Bluebeard than of Blackbeard in the tale, but to a six- or sixty-year-old it is still a lot of fun. The truth is that Blackbeard was not a nice fellow, and he was most likely a misogynist. A misogynist who loved women! Now that's one for the psychologists. It is known that he married quite a few ladies, after a fashion, and that one of his so-called widows was still alive as late as 1757 according to Edward Rowe Snow, the great pirate authority and author of more than 116 books on subjects connected with the sea and its history. All I can say is that the story makes a fine yarn.

During his years of depredation and fun, Blackbeard built himself a fleet of ships. His favorite vessel was a fine craft that he captured. He named her *Queen Anne's Revenge*. His pirate ventures were blessed with great success up and down the Atlantic Coast from New England vessels to ships taken in the Caribbean area. His treasure was so large that the thought of sharing it gave him no peace. He wanted it all. The solution to that little problem was resolved by slipping his cable and taking off with the whole thing, leaving his fellow brothers of the coast high and dry along with his fleet. This was not calculated to make Blackbeard too popular with his pirate confraternity.

Speaking of Blackbeard's friends, the circle was getting smaller, but the governor of the Carolinas was still among them. Alexander Spotswood, governor of Virginia, was decidedly not among them. In fact, he wanted to see Blackbeard brought to account for his crimes. To that end, Spotswood sent acting Lieutenant Maynard to track down the dreaded and notorious giant pirate. Maynard had two ships for this purpose and a burning desire to make good on his assignment. This was because Maynard may have been the oldest acting lieutenant in the British navy. He was passed over for promotion time and time again for his failure to grasp the basic subjects that British naval officers were expected to know. Maynard was considered to be very dull. Unlike the British army, where officers' commissions could be bought along with promotions, the navy was a meritocracy where officers actually had to know their stuff. This mission could make Maynard's future, and he knew it well. He might even make a few pounds out of the bargain.

Maynard tracked Blackbeard down and ran him aground. That is to say, Maynard and his two vessels chased Blackbeard up an inlet until all three ships involved were run aground on sandbars at low tide. Maynard attacked Blackbeard with all the fury born out of pure desperation. He just couldn't remain the oldest midshipman in the navy forever. Blackbeard fought like the devil he was until, after a long fight and an incredible number of wounds that would have killed a dozen other mere men, he just collapsed stone dead. Blackbeard's body received countless wounds inflicted by guns, cutlasses and swords. But still the giant had fought on with all of his considerable power until he just tumbled over onto the deck like a felled ox. Maynard ordered his head struck off and suspended from the prow of his ship. Full of victory, Maynard returned to port. The trophy was displayed for a while then disappeared. Maynard's reward turned out to be one pound!

Later Blackbeard's skull was obtained by a colonial Virginia college fraternity who had it silver-plated and turned into a drinking vessel by having a silver cup set into the top of the skull. For more than 140 years, Blackbeard's skull served this useful purpose. During the Civil War, it was liberated by some Union soldiers who brought it north. After 80 odd years had passed, the skull was purchased by none other than historian-author Edward Rowe Snow himself. That skull could not have had a better owner than the man who had written so much about the pirate. Blackbeard was clearly one of his favorite pirates.

Edward Rowe Snow himself was a huge man even in his later years. He was not only a published author and a most prolific writer, but also he was the best storyteller I have ever had the pleasure of knowing, be it ever so slightly. On top of that, he had a true passion for collecting. Ed also enjoyed a stint on an evening Boston television news program providing local social and nautical history lessons for the program's viewers. One day while he was at the studio, the Blackbeard skull was taken from his unlocked car where it had been sitting in a cardboard box. Ed gravely went on the news broadcast the next evening and briefly related the history of the skull in bloody detail. He then placed a curse on the skull and warned of what horrible things would happen to whoever had it if it were not returned to him in very short order. Presuming that the thieves were sorry excuses for humanity anyway, there was a chance that the curse might work. The very next day, the skull was returned to Ed's unlocked car. Human nature is human nature, and Ed knew the power of fear and intimidation.

Several years after this incident, I met Ed at a meeting of the Upton Historical Society where he presented a lecture on pirates. My friend and fellow educator Ken Wood had invited me to the meeting knowing of my deep interest in all things nautical. In the course of his presentation, Ed produced Blackbeard's skull from its box. It was an object of fascination. Later in the evening, I introduced myself to Ed, and we discussed our common nautical interest. Ed invited me to visit him someday. On one fine day, I actually got into my car and motored down to the sea and Ed's home. Here I spent an unforgettable afternoon with Ed. He showed me many wonderful items including some treasure chests with very complex locks and a three-bladed knife that had belonged to the dreaded pirate Francis L'Olonnais.

L'Olonnais used the knife to cut the beating hearts out of his victims, and then he would chew on them in a rage when he became frustrated with his victims for not revealing the location of their wealth. Sometimes he would do it just as a lesson to others or because he felt like letting off a little steam. Over the course of the afternoon, my host proposed a toast to drink out of Blackbeard's skull, and that appealed to my twenty-something imagination during that warm summer of more than forty years ago. Thinking of it still sends chills of pleasure up and down my spine. How lucky anyone was who had the good fortune to meet Edward Rowe Snow. Many lighthouse keepers knew him as the "The Flying Santa." Ed liked to fly his airplane out to the lighthouses at Christmas dressed like Santa Claus and drop off gifts for the lighthouse keepers and their families.

Blackbeard's treasure is a thing of speculation. History leads us to believe that he got quite a lot of it. Logic would dictate that it must be somewhere. If you want to go looking for it, I wish you the very best of luck. My best information indicates that treasure hunters should really look around the Isle of Shoals off the coast of Maine where Captain William Kidd and so many others were also rumored to have deposited their booty in the thin and rocky soil. Blackbeard is rumored to have buried some of his loot there. If all of these old wives' tales are true, I wonder that all of the people who have gone looking for treasure over the last three hundred years are not rich.

The other greatly famed pirate of the late seventeenth century and early eighteenth century was Captain William Kidd. Kidd predates the heyday of Blackbeard and cannot be compared to him in any way. He could not compete with the sheer nastiness of the bearded giant. William Kidd was an almost respectable sea captain in New York and New England, and he was indeed a friend of the Earl of Beaumont who was the royal governor of New York. Even King William III was an investor in the privateering venture of Captain Kidd. Beaumont gave Kidd letters of marque, which allowed the captain to capture ships of nations at war with England. Such privateers were commissioned well into the nineteenth century by most western governments to capture vessels belonging to nations with which the commissioning authority was at war. It was a very common practice. Mostly because by having privateers acting as commerce raiders against the nation's foes, it freed up a warring nation's naval ships to expand their range of options against enemy warships. Kidd was to fill this vital role of privateer as an English patriot and businessman.

Captain Kidd, aboard his ship, the *Adventure Galley*, did not enjoy much success in the privateering enterprise. In fact, he couldn't seem to find any Spanish or French ships to attack. Since Kidd's men were paid a percentage on the basis of what they caught in the line of enemy shipping, actually taking prizes was a must. Kidd was just not delivering the goods. Needless to say, his crew, over which he didn't appear to exercise much control, was not too keen on following him much longer. One member of the unhappy crew, William Moore, was far more outspoken than the rest. He attacked Kidd's manhood and his huge lack of success in such a way that Kidd lost control of himself, grabbed a heavy, ironbound, wooden bucket and caved in Moore's skull with it. The next day Moore died without having come to. Moore

Howard Pyle's depiction of Captain Kidd spinning a yarn for Governor Beaumont. From the December 1894 edition of *Harper's Magazine*.

THE YANKEE FLEET

The inhuman pirate Francois L'Olonnais showing a victim his own still-beating heart that had just been cut out of him with Edward Rowe Snow's three-bladed knife.

was one of the most popular members of the crew, and his death did not sit well with the men. By contrast, Kidd was at his most unpopular. This presented a real problem for the failed privateer. In short order, the crew presented the captain with an ultimatum which was, "Turn pirate or else!"

Kidd knew that he enjoyed no respect from his crew whatsoever and that his life, as well as his command, was now in mortal danger. The voyage had gone so badly that anything had to be better than that which he was suffering. In the face of all this, he threw in his lot with his crew and became a buccaneer. Not long after, a large prize was sighted. Kidd gave chase and came up to the ship, which proved to be the very large and very rich East Indiaman, the *Quedagh Merchant*.

To Kidd, the now Anglo-American pirate, the ship was a beauty. After a brief fight, the ship was taken. It was a very rich treasure ship indeed, but there was only one small problem. The ship had been chartered by the Great Mogul of Delhi who was an ally of the English Crown and therefore under the protection of the Royal Navy. The English government now found themselves embroiled in a huge international incident. The big ship seemed to be sailing under French papers, but that had been some sort of subterfuge that has never really been explained. Had Kidd kept and had been allowed to hang onto those French papers, he might have had a chance to save himself later on. Kidd was in every sense everybody's scapegoat. A warrant was drawn up ordering the capture of Kidd who eventually was taken into custody.

His friends in Massachusetts and New York no longer wished to know him, nor did his backers in the privateering venture. His papers were seized, and documents which might have saved him were made to vanish, not to be seen again for the better part of three centuries, the aforementioned French papers among them. Kidd argued that these French papers were proof that he had acted properly. But that didn't matter since they were among the missing papers. Everybody seemed to be out to take a pound of flesh from poor Captain Kidd. There would be no knighthood for him as there had been for Sir Henry Morgan who three decades earlier was the supreme author of piratical depredations.

Kidd was tried far from New England and New York where he had been so much at home in recent years. He was in the dock in London, charged with piracy and exceeding his commission as a privateer with letters of marque given to him by Lord Beaumont who, in turn, was made to resign as royal governor of New York in disgrace. Kidd was found guilty of the murder of the rude sailor Moore whom he had felled with that ironbound wooden bucket. There was no dispute about that. Many members of Kidd's nasty crew, who had forced him to turn pirate in the first place, gave evidence against him out of sheer spite, and poor Kidd was found guilty of piracy and sentenced to be hanged in 1701. On the day designated for his hanging, Kidd was placed in a cart and taken to his place of execution. There was a huge turnout to see the unfortunate Kidd hanging. The mob followed the cart to the execution dock with bottles of rum and other warming drinks to toast the proceedings of this grim holiday. It was the custom of celebration on hanging day—not only of that time, but right up to the end of public executions all over the western world, including the United States—that brought out the joyful rum- and gin-soaked crowds.

The noose was placed around Kidd's neck. The proper prayers were intoned. The crowd watched in expectation of the show. The trap was sprung, and Kidd was hanged. But wait! What's this? The rope snapped, and Kidd fell to the ground. The guards stood him up, and up the steps Kidd went again. Once more the rope was placed around his neck. The crowd strained to see, and Kidd was hanged again. But alas, the rope broke again. Now, there is in British constitution a law that grew out of custom and usage, and which is enshrined in *Blackstone*, that says if a man be hanged and the rope doth break three times, that man shall go free. The people watching were well up on this point of law and were no doubt laying odds and taking bets on the likelihood of Kidd pulling off this hat trick. Once again, the executioner placed a rope around Kidd's thick neck and then let him drop a third time. This time it held, and the luckless pirate, much bruised and shaken, was sent off into that land from which no person shall return. This time the executioner had used a new rope. Poor Kidd just had no luck at all.

Rumors abounded all along the colonial Atlantic Coast from the District of Maine down as far as Long Island that Kidd had landed in the black of the night to hide his treasure. Maybe he had, but not possibly in all the places, which have been reported. The poor man would never have had the time to go to England to be tried and hanged if he had actually spent all that time hiding his ill-gotten gains all over New England. For more than three hundred years since the captain was sent on to glory, New Englanders have been seeking his gold. Maybe the islands of Boston Harbor hold some of the answers to these vexing questions. After all, pirate gold has been found on those islands before. Then again, maybe a lot of it was buried on the aforementioned Isle of Shoals, but then again, maybe not.

Chapter 4

More Depraved Pirates, Buccaneers and Henpecked Rovers

Captain Kidd was a rather tame pirate by the standards set by Morgan and Blackbeard. But there were a lot of really nasty fellows who would live up to the image we have held of these brutal pirates most foul. There were a lot of men with New England connections like Edward Low, Thomas Tew, John Quelch, Sam Bellamy and even southerner Stede Bonnet who came by their savage reputations because of their depredations on the high seas. These pirates each carved out a reputation for himself that made his name a household word in his own time in New England long before the advent of mass media. Some were savage. Some were gentlemen. And here and there was an odd fellow who just wanted to get away from his nagging and abusive wife.

No pirate who prowled the waters of New England and the North Atlantic was more wretched than Edward Low. He grew up as an all but feral child in the Westminster district of London. He and his equally horrible brother grew up like two savage dogs near the London docks and the coming and going of international shipping. This included ships going to and from the colonial trading centers of British America like Boston. At his first opportunity, Edward Low worked his way aboard a ship bound for Boston, Massachusetts. After an uneventful passage, he arrived in Boston, left the ship, and as was his old habit, he became a creature of the docks and waterfront taverns. He was always on the lookout for something.

Low was uneducated and vicious. He was given to fits of rage and was not afraid to lash out with extreme violence if he were crossed or challenged in any way. After looking about for a ship, he found a place on a vessel bound for Honduras on a trading voyage. The ship departed Boston and made its way through the southern latitudes. Here in the tropical heat, the trouble began. Low was restive. He released his pent up energy by bulling the crew. His temper flared and knew no bounds. He took to pushing the mates around and even terrorized the captain himself. His fine madness was such that nobody tried to stop him as his behavior became more boldly extreme and even totally irrational. No common deckhand

The Yankee Fleet

Coins that made up pirate treasure like this real cob struck in Bolivia in 1625 and this piece of eight of 1588.

of the early eighteenth century ever had the attitude of Ned Low and was not flogged or hanged for it. No common sailor in history pulled off the flagrant acts of overt disrespect to his superiors and lived to tell about it unless they were party to a full-blown mutiny.

Flogging sailors for insubordination at that time was common practice in the British merchant service. In the navy during that period, Low would have been hanged for his behavior. But the man to flog Ned Low had not been born. Low took on the captain in a savage verbal exchange in which he totally intimidated the man. Not long after this, Low took a longboat and a small company of the ship's malcontents and set off on his own. Low's natural leadership qualities appealed to these men who elected to follow him. This longboat proved to be Low's first pirate command. Within a few days at sea, Low spied a small sailing ship. In the dark of the night, the pirates made their way aboard and fell on the ship's captain, officers and crew. Low slaughtered them all and threw their bodies overboard. Now Ned Low was the master of a real ship. He was a full-fledged pirate.

During the months that followed, he took any merchantman that had the great misfortune to come his way. Low offered the men he captured the option of joining him or being thrown to the sharks. As he sailed along, he traded up through a series of more powerful vessels. Eventually he collected together a goodly number of ships and built himself a ragtag fleet of pirate craft. With such fine natural gifts,

More Depraved Pirates, Buccaneers and Henpecked Rovers

Ned would have made a successful Wall Street corporate raider today. By 1722, his fleet of pirate ships manned by a large crew of buccaneers ranged the waters of the Atlantic from the Antilles in the south to the waters off Boston and Newfoundland in the north. Ships sailing out of Boston, where Low had first landed in America, easily fell prey to him. Most of his new crew thought going on account with Low was a profitable romp.

No doubt these lusty New England lads, having run away from the constraints of Puritan society, thought that the prospect of "going on account" was very exciting. Some men most likely thought of the wealth they could gain, and others thought that they might even get to command ships of their own. Pirates, unlike most of mankind, enjoyed a rudimentary democracy unknown in any other place on the planet. They had some very democratic rules, some of which actually constituted a contract known as ship's articles. These were set down in writing, while other rights grew out of custom and usage. Pirate captains were elected for the most part, as I have stated earlier in this narrative, and should the captain lose his courage or be less than successful, he could be deposed. Other rules covered compensation for loss of body parts such as legs, ears, arms, noses, eyes and other odd bits and pieces. Low may have been fierce, but even he could only hold command as long as he enjoyed the confidence of his men and stuck to the rules. Robert Lewis Stevenson in his classic *Treasure Island* constantly references pirate rules and rights.

For some time, Low seemed to be doing well, and he even looked after the welfare of his men in his own way. For example, when his stock of medical supplies ran out, he decided to allow the governor at St. Michael's to supply his needs. He was not unlike Blackbeard in this capacity. In fact, his tactics were pretty much the same. Low seized a number of ships coming out of the port of St. Michael, and then he sent a not-so-diplomatic note simply stating, "Give me the supplies that I requested, or I'll burn all of your ships. If you do as I wish, your ships will be returned unharmed."

Knowing of Low's reputation as a man with a very low tolerance, not to mention less than traditional humanitarian impulses, the governor sent the supplies as requested. Water and other provisions were sent out to the pirates along with the medicine chest. Captain Ned was as good as his word in this instance. The ships and crews he had taken were released unharmed. This strategic victory over authority seemed to boost Low's courage to new heights. Low next decided to attack an English man-of-war with his fleet.

Having sighted a likely foe, he attacked with his customary ferocity and bravado. Initially the battle seemed lopsided, but the vastly outnumbered English vessel, with its highly disciplined crew and superior gunnery, made short work of most of the pirate fleet. Seeing that mere bluster could not defeat the Royal Navy, Low tucked tail and fled the battle. At least one of the pirate vessels was captured, and the rest of his ships fled or limped away. The captured pirate ship and its unlucky crew were taken back to Rhode Island for trial. The pirate gang was thrown on the gentle mercies of that colony's justice system. The merchants of the colony were not very sympathetic to Low's men. The buccaneers were charged with piracy, tried, found guilty of their crimes and sentenced to be hanged. On appeal, a third of those facing death proved to the satisfaction of the authorities that they had been forced to join Low on pain of death. Given Low's well-known character, the court relented and agreed that the men had been "forced." The other two-thirds were hanged. Low, on hearing of this, went quite mad with rage.

He vowed revenge and rebuilt his fleet and recruited more men. Low attacked New England shipping with more abandon than any time before. He then sailed from Boston down to the Antilles and then back again to the Boston waters before moving up to Newfoundland. His anger became more intense. Low's anger was the greatest when directed against somebody who had hidden their wealth on a ship he captured, or even worse, had thrown their riches overboard. He hanged these poor wretches from the masts and yardarms just at a height at which he could still reach them and flayed the living flesh from their bones with his sword. Even his own men found him to be totally barbaric and beastly.

At the top of his game, Low styled himself "Admiral of the Fleet." He went so far as to create a flag for all his vessels to fly. It featured a red skull on a black background. According to Charles Johnson, one of the earliest writers on the subject of seventeenth- and early eighteenth-century piracy, Low and his second in command had a falling out over some scheme of the pirate's trade. The discussion was animated and became general knowledge to the ship's community. At last, the crew openly took the mate's part in the dispute. Low grew silent. During the rest of the day the ship was still, and Low kept to his quarters. He was not accustomed to being crossed. After night had fallen and most of the crew had turned in for the night, Low exacted his revenge. In the dark of night, he went to where his mate was sleeping, and killed him for opposing him before the crew.

Low had forgotten the democracy of piracy. This was not one of his majesty's ships of war, and the captain, or even an admiral, of a pirate fleet was not a law unto himself. When the murder was discovered the following day, it was the crew's turn to be enraged. After a loud exchange of yelling and oaths, Admiral Edward Low was deposed as pirate chief, and another leading member of the company was elected to take his place. Knowing what a dangerous man Low was, not to mention that he was more than just a tad mad, it was agreed to place him and his two remaining loyalists in an open boat without provisions and set them adrift on the high seas. Now to be shoved off in an unprovisioned boat with a man so dedicated to self-preservation as Ned Low had its own troubling implications, such as ending up as his lunch should he become unduly peckish. Not to mention perversely hungry.

Just after Captain Low's ship disappeared over the horizon, another ship came into view and spotted the deposed pirate admiral and the sailors in distress. Within a few hours, Low and his confederates were rescued. The presumption was that the men in the boat had survived a ship's sinking. They were told that the rescue ship was bound for Martinique a few days' sail away. Low played his hand well. He even managed to control his natural impulses (which was amazing since today he would most definitely be diagnosed with impulse control disorder) and remained somewhat civil for the duration of the voyage. He might even have smiled once or twice.

Ned Low had been handed a second chance at life. No doubt he passed many happy hours keeping his own council and planning a horrible revenge of unsurpassed and savage sweetness against those men who dared to depose their admiral. At last, the rescue ship reached the beautiful island of Martinique. Upon landing, Low wasted no time in looking for his next vessel and gave some thought to putting together a new crew. But about this time he was recognized, and it was "Voilà! C'est Ned Low!" He and his two companions were taken into custody.

The governor of the French colony was pleased that the great Ned Low was now in his power, and being a practical man, the governor wasted no time in rendering Ned harmless. The governor disposed of his guest tout de suite, which was most likely a very good idea. In 1724, Ned's head paid the price for all his crimes. His tortured and twisted life ended on one of the most beautiful islands in the world. Boston would never know Ned Low again.

If Ned Low was uncouth, vicious and mean, Thomas Tew was a refined gentleman of great polish. In 1734, pirate historian Charles Johnson wrote of him, "Thomas Tew in point of gallantry was second to none." This was high praise for a fellow known as "The Rhode Island Pirate." Tew was actually born not in Rhode Island but in Northamptonshire, England, in the days of the Cromwellian Commonwealth. As an upper middle-class adult, he migrated to Rhode Island and settled in the vicinity of Newport. As a member of the local gentry, he entered the social circle of Rhode Island's Governor Benjamin Fletcher. By now Tew had married and had fathered a daughter.

By the late 1690s, England was once again at war with the French and Spanish. This time it was over the throne of Spain whose idiot king, Charles II, had no heir, and the throne was offered to the grandson of Louis XIV of France. The English found this an intolerable situation because it gave the Sun King, Louis XIV, too much power in European and thus world affairs. The natural result was the War of the Spanish Succession. France's fleet would now be joined by Spain's fleet against English interests all over the world, including the Americas. As a result, letters of marque would be issued to Tew just as they had been to Captain Kidd. Tew saw a chance for fortune, and he decided to go privateering. He looked forward to raising a crew, arming a ship and taking rich prizes. It proved to be no problem. With Tew being a close friend of the governor, nothing could follow but success. Tew became a privateer with Fletcher's blessing. For the next several years, Tew took many Spanish and French prizes all quite within the law. But during this period, it also occurred to him that richer pickings existed in the Indian Ocean. Alas, greed reared its ugly head, and that vast ocean, far to the east, called to him from half a world away, from the Atlantic, which he had plundered so well and with such distinguished style.

The Yankee Fleet

Howard Pyle's *So the Treasure Was Divided*. From the July 1890 edition of *Harper's Magazine*.

Fletcher and the Rhode Island crowd were under the impression that Tew was off again in chase of the enemies of William III, but he and his men clearly had other notions. Captain Tew and company, now enjoying the freedom of sail and the vast open ocean, had decided to go on account and do a bit of freebooting for fun and profit. Tew told his friend Fletcher that he wanted to move to the paradise island of Bermuda for the climate and the beauty of the place. Fletcher wished him well, and Tew resettled his family in his new island home in 1692. It was a true paradise, and his bride and daughter seemed well satisfied. Captain Tew was now ready for his new venture. Tew set sail for the Indian Ocean and the rich rewards he expected to reap.

Since the cultivated Rhode Islander had decided to turn pirate, he also decided that he needed a flag of his very own to sail under. Tew came up with a most original design. It consisted of a brawny arm with a sword in its hand posed as if ready to strike. The arm and sword were white and superimposed on a sable or black background. When Captain Tew was asked what the symbol meant, he simply answered, "It means that we are willing to kill you." Of course Tew would have preferred a ship just come about and surrender rather than go through the bothersome process of a fight to the death. He believed that a nice, uncomplicated surrender was far better than the vulgar and sweaty business of actual bloody combat. But, he was up to that too if that was what was needed. Tew was always ready to oblige the combative. Before too long Tew's fame as a pirate began to grow, and Captain William Kidd, as King William's man in that part of the world, was commissioned to capture or kill him. It is funny and ironic that Captain Kidd was sent to capture Tew since he would become a pirate within a short time himself. In fact, Kidd did set out to find Tew, but events would prevent them from ever meeting.

One fine day, Tew encountered a well-appointed ship belonging to the Great Mogul of Delhi, the *Fatch*. Tew thought that it would make a fine prize and a

More Depraved Pirates, Buccaneers and Henpecked Rovers

grand flagship for a little pirate fleet with which to return to his base that he had just founded along with his new friend, Captain Mission. Mission was a fairly well-known French pirate with a bit of refined breeding himself. Their town was called Libertalia. The name reflected their philosophy of joy in living a free life outside of the constraints of man's law. Strangely they regarded their honor as something of profound importance.

Tew hailed the *Fatch*, but she refused to come about and surrender peacefully. Tew had no choice but to fall on her and attack. Catching up with the *Fatch*, he fired some shots and then went aboard her. He and his crew engaged in battle. He sought to overawe the foe with the fierceness of his attack, but it was Tew who was outmatched this time. As hard as he fought, things did not go well for Captain Tew and his men. At last, fighting against impossible odds, the gentleman pirate was killed. His career was ended before he could meet Captain Kidd in battle. Had Tew actually met Kidd, I wonder if he could have charmed the privateer into joining him in a pirate's life before Kidd's own men had forced his hand in that direction. It's one of those historic speculations.

If Thomas Tew was a gentleman, John Quelch was not. This very evil pirate designed a flag that suited his personality and gave insight into his character or lack thereof. It consisted of a naked albino male holding an hourglass in his left hand and a spear in his right, which in turn stabbed a human heart. This whole ghastly motif was superimposed on a black background. The John Quelch story of piracy begins in Boston, Massachusetts, in the early 1700s. A number of Boston merchants were set to take advantage of the international situation, now known as the War of the Spanish Succession, and outfit a privateer. For this purpose they bought a good ship named the *Charles*.

The Boston merchants next named an able skipper by the name of David Plowman as master of the *Charles*. As it happened, Plowman fell ill and sent word to the investors to come down to the ship to meet with him and judge for themselves his condition for continued command. He knew that delay would cost them dearly, and being a good Puritan of deep religious conviction, he did not want to cheat them. Plowman thought it best to leave the decision in their hands as to whether he would stay in command or whether he would be relieved of command in favor of a healthy captain. Plowman also communicated that there was a real problem with the crew. He stated in his letter that he did not trust them. His fears were very well founded.

Shortly after the letter from the captain was sent, seaman Quelch and the crew hoisted sail and took the *Charles* out of Boston Harbor. After the *Charles* cleared the port of Boston, Quelch and his henchmen entered Plowman's cabin and took the protesting captain onto the deck and heaved him overboard. On hearing of the ship's sudden departure, Governor Thomas Dudley, suspecting that something was not right, expressed extreme displeasure over the *Charles*'s leaving. The investors shared the governor's feelings and fears. Plowman's letter had set warning bells off in

A type of vessel favored by pirates for conversion to their trade.

their heads. They all knew that Plowman would never have set out in his weakened physical condition. They sensed that something was terribly wrong.

Efforts to find the *Charles* failed. Aboard the ship, all thoughts of privateering were abandoned by the crew in favor of something more adventurous. Quelch had turned the men of the *Charles,* and they had elected to turn pirate and go on account. Quelch was elected captain by acclamation and became Captain Quelch in 1703. He did not limit his exploits to just Spanish and French ships, but sought ships of all nations as prizes. No merchant ship was safe from Quelch, not even those of England's oldest ally in Europe, Portugal. Dozens of Portuguese ships fell prey to the *Charles*, which was a very fast and strong ship well suited to its new calling.

Quelch had taken in quite a haul during his spree of pirating before the *Charles* set course for Marblehead for much-needed provisions. When the *Charles* sailed into port, it was boarded in force by the authorities who wasted no time in confronting Captain Quelch in regard to his voyage. They had a special interest in the fate of Captain Plowman. Quelch told the officials that Captain Plowman, with brave and total disregard for his own health, had ordered the ship to sea. Quelch said that

More Depraved Pirates, Buccaneers and Henpecked Rovers

Plowman was very anxious to start taking as many French and Spanish ships as possible in as little time as he could manage. According to the pirate chief, Plowman grew increasingly sick each day and at last died.

Quelch then went on to say that the captain was buried at sea with all the ceremonies the ship could provide. He said that he was forced by the circumstances of the voyage to take command of the vessel himself. He lamented all the misadventures to date and wrung his hands with the sorrows of the heavy burdens that were thrust upon him by the unfortunate circumstances of the privateering adventure gone awry. A search of the vessel revealed a great deal of Portuguese gold and silver and other coin. The authorities asked Quelch where it had come from. He replied that most of it had been taken from the wreck of a Spanish galleon which they had been most fortunate to find.

The authorities thought that this information was strange, and a search was conducted anew. This time the crew was questioned more closely. These poor lads lacked Quelch's imagination and wits. Slowly, bit by bit, the truth emerged as the crew was broken down under the hammering of the unrelenting Puritans. All aboard were held in close confinement until Governor Dudley could sort it all out. It did not take him very long to do so, and he ordered the arrest of Quelch and the whole crew.

Unfortunately for this unhappy mob, the Commonwealth of Massachusetts Bay had just passed a new pirate law. Quelch and his crew had the singular distinction of being the very first pirates tried under its provisions. It was to be a sort of show trial, and Massachusetts Bay Colony was loaded for bear. The trial itself was held in one of the largest venues of Boston, the Star Tavern on Hanover Street. The proceedings were short and sweet. Quelch and nineteen of his men were tried, found guilty of murder and piracy and sentenced to be hanged. It was generally thought to be a just verdict and judgment for the crimes committed, including the brutal murder of Captain Plowman and acts of piracy. Two of the crew were later let off. One lad was excused because of his extreme youth, and the other was pardoned because of grave illness. He was just too sick to be hanged poor fellow.

Quelch was just an uncouth thug, but Bartholomew Roberts was "the Dandy Pirate." He dressed like someone out of a Gilbert and Sullivan production. He plied his trade off the New England coast, as well as the southern colonies. He could also be found off the coast of Newfoundland, the southern coast of Africa and around the Indies. He was also styled "the Great Roberts" or "the Great Pirate Roberts" because he seemed to enjoy effortless success at his trade. Roberts was tall and very handsome, and almost everybody seemed to like him. He really was a storybook pirate. He did kill some people, but unlike Blackbeard, he really didn't enjoy that aspect of his calling. Roberts dressed in a crimson velvet waistcoat and breeches. He also wore a diamond encrusted gold cross about his neck suspended from a gold chain. His wide-brimmed hat featured a deep red plume. He cut quite a romantic figure. He was the best of bad men. He was Hollywood before there was Hollywood. Roberts also had a rare form of courage and panache. Today it would be called attitude. Whatever it was, it was real. His flare for the dramatic made him fun to watch and hear stories about. Stories were published about his exploits, and stories flew from port to port up and down the whole Atlantic Coast.

His flare for the dramatic was best shown by an exploit he pulled off as he sailed into the harbor at Trepassey, Newfoundland. There the Great Pirate Roberts, in his fancy crimson, entered the harbor with his sword by his side, gun ports open in his ten-gun sloop, drums beating to quarters, trumpets blasting and his sixty men armed to the teeth and brandishing their weapons on the deck. Such was the terror of this bold and daring act that the crews of twenty-two ships in the harbor all abandoned their vessels and fled to the shore. These ships were plundered each in its turn. Then Roberts sailed away. It is thought that Roberts learned his sailing skills in the Royal Navy as a common sailor. There is no doubt that he was very smart and used the navy as his university of seamanship.

Roberts was truly amazing, but the end comes to us all and to pirates faster than most. The twenty-nine-year-old folk hero, for that is what he became, met his death off the coast of Africa in 1719 when his ship ran afoul of one of his majesty's ships of war. The battle commenced shortly after the two vessels sighted one another, and Roberts was hit by a stray shot during the savage fight. Fate did not permit him to show off his amazing swordplay that day. It was all quite unfair. His men, who had followed him out of love and respect, threw his body overboard so that his handsome head could not be displayed, as Blackbeard's had, like some obscene trophy. The British could not make sport of him in death as Roberts did of them in life.

A pirate's life was not a long one. Their careers were short, but even by pirate standards, Black Sam Bellamy's was very short indeed. In point of fact, he didn't even last a single year. But during that time, he took more than fifty ships. His fantastic pirating on such an impressive scale deeply affected commerce in New England. In spite of all his great success, in his brief span of being a pirate, Bellamy became known for his extreme kindness and compassion. This did not make him well loved in Boston however. He really liked taking ships without hurting anyone. He was also known for being very polite. His mercy and generosity to his captives were as legendary as his exploits. His crew even called themselves "Robin Hood's Band." They called their captain "Prince of Pirates."

Bellamy was very young when he ventured to Massachusetts from England in his pre-pirating days. He landed at Cape Cod, and shortly thereafter, he fell in love with a girl there. She was a young country girl of some wealth by the name of Maria Hallet. Maria was instantly attracted to Black Sam Bellamy. It truly was love at first sight. He was handsome (he most likely had all of his teeth, which was a big plus in those days), and he wore his hair long and naturally black, hence the nickname Black Sam. After a while, Sam convinced Maria that their fortune was to be found in the

More Depraved Pirates, Buccaneers and Henpecked Rovers

sunny south off Spanish Florida in the business of recovering treasure from Spanish ships that had met a sorry end. He then introduced Maria to his financial backer in the treasure recovery scheme, one Paul Williams. After talking with the two men at length, Maria decided that the venture had very good prospects of success.

After some time and a lot of work on the salvage project, Sam decided that maybe the venture was a mistake after all. The work was far from easy and not at all profitable. Sam was very discouraged. It now seemed that there was only one alternative career possible. Piracy! Sam went on account and linked up with a friend of Blackbeard by the name of Captain Benjamin Horngold. Horngold commanded the good ship *Mary Anne*. Apparently Horngold did not please his crew, for in 1716, they deposed him. This coup was led by Sam Bellamy, who stood for captain himself and was elected by a great majority vote. Horngold was out, and young Black Sam Bellamy was in. One of the first acts of piracy that Captain Bellamy engaged in was the taking of a ship much to his liking by the name of *Sultana*. He kept the ship as his own personal command. In this fine vessel, he sailed off into pirating immortality.

Between 1716 and 1717, Bellamy captured more than fifty ships and their cargoes. That was a fantastic achievement by any standard. One of the last ships he took was the truly fine vessel the *Whydah*. There was something about that ship that just appealed to Bellamy and his men. The Prince of Pirates and his merry men loved it at first sight. The captain of the *Whydah* was informed by Bellamy that he intended to take his ship along with its cargo. No doubt the poor man wondered what he was going to do without a vessel to take him back to England. He had the experience of knowing what most other pirates would do, but here he was dealing with a different breed of freebooter altogether. He was amazed by what Bellamy next proposed.

Bellamy unloosed a real shocker. He told the Captain of the *Whydah* that he could have the *Sultana*, which was also a very trim craft, and such provisions as he needed to return to England with all of his men. The captain of the *Whydah* could hardly believe his good fortune. When he made it back to England and told his story about the kind pirate, it could hardly be believed. Bellamy's generosity was not typical pirate behavior at the time. Corporate raiders of today could take a lesson from Bellamy and show a little mercy every now and then. The voyage had been a great success. Now Sam just wanted to get back to Maria. To that end, he charted a course for Cape Cod.

Bellamy headed back to the beautiful woman he loved. As he sailed north, the weather seemed to get worse. The winds blew very fresh, and the skies darkened. There was no out sailing what was to come next. He was almost home, yet the longest miles of his life existed between him and what he wanted most in the world, Maria. Maybe Bellamy wondered if he should sail into the wind and stand out to sea to weather the blast that was to come upon him. We will never know what Sam thought at the moment that the great hurricane of 1717 struck with all of its awesome fury. The *Whydah* must have been tossed like a child's plaything as it fought to stay afloat. The angry Atlantic, ever hungry for poor little ships and seamen,

An eighteenth-century pirate on his way to the gallows as depicted in the July 1890 edition of *Harper's Magazine*.

swallowed the ship and all of its crew as well. There was nobody left to tell the tale of what the last thoughts of the men on that doomed ship were. All of the *Whydah's* ill-gotten treasure could not buy even one life of all those aboard. Just a short way off Wellfleet, Massachusetts, 144 men were lost on that ship. So passed the kindest of pirates in the year of 1717.

Bellamy was gone, never to know the sweet embrace of his darling Maria, but he was not forgotten. After 267 years had passed, Barry Clifford and his friends capped off a long search and found the bones of the unfortunate *Whydah* off the shores of Wellfleet. This exciting discovery made international news. At the time of its sinking, the *Whydah* was carrying a rich cargo of indigo (a desirable blue die), ivory, gold and thirty thousand pounds sterling in coin. The value of the coins alone, in terms of 2007 dollars, would be in the vicinity of $4.5 million in face value. The numismatic value of the coins may be many times greater depending on the preservation of the coins themselves. But the real value of any wreck of that antiquity must be in its history and the historic importance of its artifacts. Artifacts from Bellamy's last ship can be seen today at the museum set up by Barry Clifford in Provincetown, Massachusetts.

Sam Bellamy loved his Maria and died attempting to return to her, but Major Stede Bonnet would rather have died than spend one more day with his nagging scold

More Depraved Pirates, Buccaneers and Henpecked Rovers

of a wife. His history overlaps with that of New England even though he spent most of his life in the sunny climate of the Carolinas. Poor Bonnet was as badly a henpecked man as was ever wedded to a bona fide witch. He was really driven to piracy to get away from his shrew of a wife who made his life a living hell. Bonnet was a rich southern planter living in the same time period as Blackbeard and the rest of the pirates of the Golden Age of Piracy. I guess that it was a golden age if you were a pirate. Most merchants all up and down the Atlantic would disagree that it was a golden age for them because it was their gold that gave that age its name. Sea captains who carried rich cargoes might have called the time period something else.

Bonnet's wife had such a savage tongue that he lied to her and said that he wanted to leave their plantation to try his hand at being an island trader. The prospect of even more income led her to agree to the separation for an extended time. I suppose that she could while away her time abusing her servants and slaves in Stede's absence. Bonnet was in his middle years and was having the granddaddy of all midlife crises. He was well educated, landed and a respected community leader who unlike most pirates actually bought his own ship. He called it the *Revenge*. Sigmund Freud could have had a lot of fun with Bonnet's choice of name for his ship. It mounted ten guns and was a very sturdy vessel. Bonnet sailed it off to Barbados and enjoyed some success in taking prizes. It seems that it didn't take him long to get a feel for his new trade.

He then sailed up the coast to New England to try his luck. He captured enough Massachusetts and Connecticut ships to cause some serious concerns for the colonial authorities there. Before things could get too hot up north for him, Bonnet sailed south again to the happier hunting grounds of the Barbados. For some unknown reason, it seems that Bonnet developed a real hatred for the merchants of the Barbados. When he took their ships, he burned them instead of just stripping them and sending them on their way. Needless to say, that was not his usual method of operation.

It was about this time that one of the strangest friendships in history was born. Stede Bonnet met the king of the pirates, Blackbeard, in 1717, and a friendship developed between the refined gentleman pirate and the wild sociopath. Blackbeard admired Bonnet's cultivation and education. I suspect that Bonnet liked the way Blackbeard treated his wives and collection of tarts. Whatever it was that bound these two together, Blackbeard remained loyal to his friend even after he removed Bonnet from the command of his ship.

In the beginning of their professional relationship, Blackbeard proposed to Bonnet that they enter into a joint pirate venture and make a fortune or two. Bonnet agreed. In fact, Bonnet was flattered that the famed Blackbeard wanted to join forces with him in the first place. But after watching his friend in battle, Blackbeard knew that Bonnet would be a liability. Bonnet may have had some military background, but this landlubber was no real sailor. He was just a slightly gifted amateur in

The Yankee Fleet

Blackbeard's world. One day, Blackbeard invited Bonnet to parley aboard the *Adventure Galley*, which was one of his favorite flagships in a whole line of them. Once Bonnet arrived on board and was placed in the best cabin, which had been made as plush as possible, Blackbeard told his friend some unpleasant truths. Namely, Bonnet was told that he was no pirate, at least not up to Blackbeard's exacting standards. Blackbeard went on to tell Bonnet that he was too refined a gentleman to command a ship in the pirate fleet, and that he should just sit back on the *Adventure Galley* and enjoy the show.

This is not what Bonnet had in mind when he threw in his lot with Blackbeard, but at least Blackbeard wasn't shooting him or nagging him to death. In fact, the big pirate was the perfect host. Life aboard the ship was still much better than at home. Bonnet was a prisoner in a sort of plush-lined, gold-plated cage. Blackbeard dined with him and showed Bonnet every mark of respect. Meanwhile, the command of *Revenge* had been handed to one of Blackbeard's most trusted lieutenants, a man named Richards. The threat of a loyalist uprising against Richards loomed on Bonnet's ship, but Richards had learned his lessons in command well under Blackbeard. A few growls and a raised bushy eyebrow were enough to discourage any potential mutiny. Bonnet's crew was whipped into shape in quick order. After a few months had passed, Bonnet was successful in persuading Blackbeard into letting him sail off on his own account as master of the restored *Revenge*. I can just see Blackbeard in a rare moment of humanity saying to Bonnet, "All right lad, just don't hurt yourself. Do take care, and don't forget to write."

The truth was that by this point Stede Bonnet was sick and tired of the roving life. He sailed back to the Carolinas, and threw himself on the mercy of Governor Charles Eden. Eden proved to be sympathetic. His private thoughts must have been, "This is the worse case of midlife crisis I've ever seen."

Bonnet was slapped on the wrist, told to go forth and sin no more, and to get home to his ever-loving wife. Bonnet's wife was hopping mad, and she made it quite clear to him that things were going to change. Life with Blackbeard was beginning to look somewhat more ideal in retrospect. After a brief interval on the old home plantation, Bonnet suddenly decided to return to sea. He now resolved to abandon his plantation along with his harpy bride forever. Eden was now beside himself with rage on learning of Bonnet's return to piracy. The governor was not having any of it. Bonnet's behavior was worse than merely than that of a gentleman breaking his word. He was downright un-English! This time there would be no pardon. Eden sent out a first-class pirate catcher, Colonel William Rhett, to retrieve the backsliding Bonnet. This time Stede Bonnet would be brought to the bar of justice.

Rhett's hunt was blessed by good fortune. He captured Bonnet before he could do too much harm to the merchants of the Barbados, but Bonnet, once caught, escaped. Rhett was not very amused by this. Piracy was a serious business, and this gifted amateur could not be allowed to undermine the law. By now Blackbeard's head was hanging from the prow of Lieutenant Maynard's ship, just to make that very judicial point. Before too long, Rhett took Bonnet for a second time. This time there would be no escape. Rhett sailed back to Charleston with Bonnet safely confined aboard ship. There would be no second chance of an elopement back to the old life on the bounding Atlantic and a subsequent return to pirating. There would be no slap on the wrist, or a trip back to the old plantation. Stede Bonnet was tried before Judge Sir Nicholas Trott Esquire for crimes of piracy, found guilty and sentenced to be hanged until dead on December 12, 1718. I am sure that Stede smiled. At least he didn't have to go home.

A pirate's life was a short one, filled with danger, and in every respect hard. But then, so was life ashore. Still, one would have to be quite desperate to leave the relative safety of the shore to go a'roving. The Golden Age of Piracy off the American Atlantic Coast ended about the time of Blackbeard's death. The mass hanging of Quelch and his nineteen comrades was just the beginning of a massive crackdown on the brothers of the coast. The British navy and colonial officials would exterminate piracy during the next decade or so. There might be the odd pirate afloat, but nothing like the masses of them that plagued the Atlantic Coast in the early 1700s.

Chapter 5

MERCHANTS AND BLOODY AMERICANS BEFORE THE REVOLUTION

After the deaths of Blackbeard, Tew, Low, Quelch, Roberts, Bellamy and other pirates, the Golden Age of Piracy was just about over as a major maritime problem in the eighteenth century. Colonial merchant shipping flourished. Three-masted ships, sloops and coastal vessels of all sorts carried various cargoes among the colonies and England. The vessels in the northern colonies moved in and out of the ports of Boston, Salem, Portsmouth, Providence, Newport and other parts of New England. One of the products shipped to England was the great timbers used to mast, spar and generally rig out the ships of the Royal Navy.

England's "walls of wood" were all that stood between the country and its growing empire that was beginning to span the globe and its imperial and commercial rivals, not to mention the fleets and the standing armies of European powers that cast a greedy eye on the island kingdom. It seems that England and France had been at war off and on ever since John Lackland was forced to sign the Magna Carta in 1215 in order to get his barons to fight the French invaders.

The Royal Navy was so determined to protect England's future that it sent crown agents into the forests of New England and the rest of the colonies to mark the tallest, straightest and largest trees with the Broad Arrow of the Royal Navy to indicate that these trees were official Crown property. Anyone who harvested such a tree was in deep trouble with the royal authorities. Americans, who by now were very independent individuals, cut them down anyway. They didn't consider the fact that they had a vested interest in the British naval ships that still protected them. As a result, British officials would enter American colonial houses and remove boards of a certain width with crowbars. The crown agents would then proceed to take these forbidden boards away and fine the transgressors. The creative American response to this was to cut wide boards into two or three narrower boards. One of the negative impacts of American control of the colonies after the American Revolution was that the British could not harvest the trees needed for masting the fleet. Denied tall, fresh sap-filled masts, the masts of the British men of war at sea would often

A typical merchant vessel of the 1740s. Featured in an old print from a drawing by Paul Egrede showing a sea serpent sighting off the coast of Massachusetts.

snap in a stiff wind. The life of a ship's mast in the eighteenth century was only ten years or so. The pine would dry out, and the mast would become too brittle to stand up to the stress of strong gales. During Britain's reign over the American colonies, remasting ships, even at sea, had not been a problem because Britain had access to the best stands of tall, straight pine in the world.

England had used up its great forests over the centuries as had much of Europe. Most European nations were disinclined to help their great commercial rival in this regard anyway. England, which had long been denuded of good stands of pine, could clearly see that Scandinavia and the rest of Europe provided little or no hope. The English began making composite masts with a round tree in the center, which would then be surrounded with four or more long, wedge-shaped pieces of wood that were in turn bound with great iron hoops to hold the entire pieced mast together. These productions were not as satisfactory as masts made entirely of one large and straight tree.

Between 1763 and 1773, Parliament passed a long string of acts including the Proclamatory Act, Sugar Act, Stamp Act, Declaratory Act, Townshend Acts, Tea Act, Port Bill and Quartering Act, which were all calculated to show the colonists who was boss, and which all, in the end, resulted in the Americans declaring their independence from Britain. What Americans resented most was being told what to do by a very remote government on a little island that seemed to lack all understanding

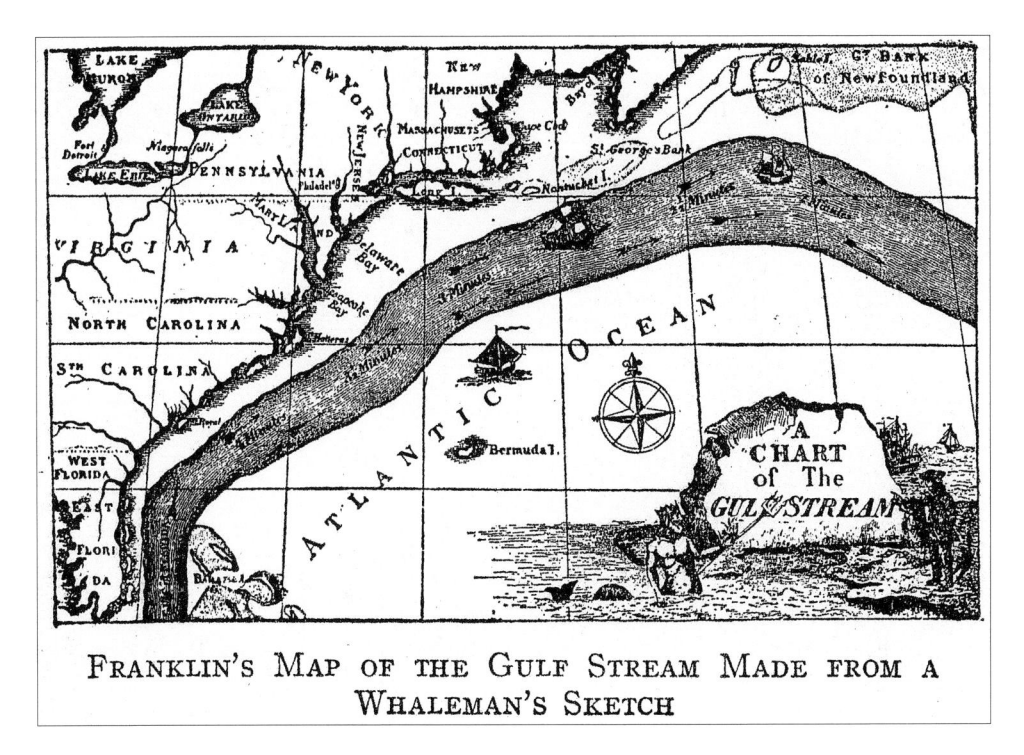

Merchants and Bloody Americans Before the Revolution

FRANKLIN'S MAP OF THE GULF STREAM MADE FROM A WHALEMAN'S SKETCH

Benjamin Frankin's map of the Gulf Stream made navigation easier in the 1760s.

of the people they governed. The acts passed by Parliament were considered as obnoxious as the acts of navigation and trade during the Commonwealth period of more than a century before, which constituted the first English attempt to control American trade. The colonials already saw themselves as something more than mere transplanted Englishmen.

In turn, the English were fearful that their North American colonies would eclipse the mother country in trade. New Englanders were building ships with their seemingly never-ending supply of fine timber. The colonists were also building more refined ships than the British shipbuilders. In contravention of the law going back to 1733, the colonists were trading for sugar in Cuba instead of British Jamaica. The British were bent on stopping this violation. The American answer was smuggling. Sugar trading in American ships wasn't important just because Americans had a sweet tooth—molasses was made from sugar and rum was distilled from sugar cane. And rum made the world go 'round, sometimes anyway, and Yankees liked it—for trade as well as for drinking purposes. Spanish Cuban sugar was cheaper and better than that of Jamaica and that is all there was to it. The British had tried to impose both the Molasses Act and, thirty-one years later, the Sugar Act on their unwilling American subjects. Both were ignored. Yankee ships kept right on bringing in those contraband cargoes under American sail and in total defiance of the law.

Tardieu L'Aine's early copperplate engraving of his antislavery print *Black Man Hanged Alive by His Ribs*.

Merchants and Bloody Americans Before the Revolution

Sugar was not the only trade in which New Englanders made a lot of money. There was also the trade in black ivory, slaves. Although New Englanders did not use slaves to the number that the southern colonists did, many built their family wealth on the African slave trade. Substantial fortunes were made in this despicable trade in human lives. Many a good Christian sea captain and his good Christian partners had ships crossing to Africa to pick up a rich cargo of humans. They sailed to the slave factories run by Europeans, American expatriates and Africans themselves, all of whom sold men, women and children away from their homelands and loved ones. Africans were crowded aboard Yankee ships bound for slave markets in the Americas.

The subdued human cargo was crammed onto these fast and fine ships three layers deep on platforms in the 'tween deck area of the merchantmen. Once every day or so, the slaves would be brought up onto the deck for exercise so the 'tween decks could be swept of human waste and the dead bodies, which were collected and thrown overboard to the waiting jaws of sharks that often attached themselves to slave ships. The merchants figured that if only a quarter to a half of the cargo died, a good profit would be entered into the ledgers. This would please the investors who could then go to mandatory Sunday worship to thank God for their good fortune. Many Yankee fortunes were made in this disgusting and unethical trade, which is a sad fact of the nautical history of New England. Most of the markets for slaves were in the southern and middle parts of colonial British America, but New England, New York and Quaker Pennsylvania also had some slaves. The Yankees dealt in the majority of this trade. Many a fine, white, Yankee church was built with the proceeds, in part at least, of this trade. According to Lerone Bennett, author of *Before the Mayflower*, more than a few churches owned slaves. In fact the Reverend Samuel Parris of Salem Village owned two slaves. One of the slaves, Tituba, was the individual who fired the imaginations of the village girls with the magic that began the town's witchcraft delusion in 1692.

Newport, Boston, Salem, Portsmouth and Philadelphia all had fine cabinetmakers, like Goddard, Townsend and Randolph, whose work could be found all over the world. Famed expert on American furniture Leigh Keno and a friend found a most exciting American secretary desk in Argentina not so long ago that could be classified among the finest pieces of American furniture ever made. Such treasures were carried to very exotic places in the age of sail. It was rumored that one southern Confederate was so totally disgusted with the outcome of the Civil War that he packed up his nearest and dearest and sailed away to Argentina in 1865. It is suggested that this fellow might also have brought all of his best heirloom furniture with him as the ultimate reminder of the better antebellum days. Among these treasures was most likely the desk that Leigh Keno found in Argentina. It's a grand story and a grand adventure. Leslie and Leigh Keno were two of the most exceptional thirteen-year-olds I had ever met back in 1969. Since that time, they

The Yankee Fleet

Leslie Keno is seen in this photograph next to the fabulous desk that a friend discovered for him in Argentina, which they in turn brought back to the United States.

have become the very faces of serious American antique collecting. This fact was even recognized by the president of the United States when he presented medals to the Kenos in honor of their scholastic contributions to the study of Americana through their writings, lecturing, participation in the *Antiques Road Show* and their own television effort, *Find*. The fact that Leigh turned up this desk in such a remote place clearly shows the trade and shipping patterns of early American furniture during the age of sail. In my opinion, that desk has got to be one of the best pieces of American furniture in existence.

American furniture of the eighteenth and early nineteenth centuries can be found in England today. Even on the island of Mauritius in the Indian Ocean, great pieces of Massachusetts tiger maple furniture have been found. Americans were just on the verge of sailing all around the world, and this was very alarming to the English. America was also importing a lot of goods from England. Ironmen in wooden ships under Yankee sail were carrying larger and larger percentages of those goods that America desired and that America sold. Many colonials like George Washington employed agents to buy clothes, wine, books and other items for them. Washington was one of several individuals who felt that substandard British goods were being fobbed off on him by his agent, to whom he fired off several angry letters on that very subject. Many colonies had agents in England to look out for their interests. Benjamin Franklin represented Pennsylvania and other colonies in this regard.

English ships brought many goods to the colonists, including: brass candlestick holders, brass bed warmers, tools of all kinds, glass, painters' colors, tea, books, furniture, wine, cloth, clothes, paper, wigs, swords, firearms and a wide variety of other items not generally made in the colonies. The English had embarked on the Industrial Revolution and had embraced the economic philosophy known as mercantilism. This economic philosophy was the brainchild of Jean Colbert, Louis XIV's minister of finance. He was in charge of all things fiscal in the French government. His 1673 concept of mercantilism was that a European nation's colonial possessions existed only to supply the mother country with raw materials and to serve as a market for the mother country's finished goods, thus keeping the balance of trade in favor of the mother country. A primary example of this would be the cotton crops of the deep southern colonies. Raw cotton would be sent to England, turned into cloth and then sold back to the colonists at a good profit.

The Industrial Revolution began in England in the manufacturing of textiles, and American cotton was needed to supply the factories of Leeds, Liverpool and other manufacturing centers of the British Isles. The plans for the textile machinery used during the Industrial Revolution were not allowed out of the country, as America was not meant to be anything more than a market for the finished cloth. In England's view, America was not ever to be the manufacturer of it. This again was mercantilism at work. The great Scottish economist Adam Smith would make a cat's dinner of this antiquated economic doctrine with his seminal work on economics, *Wealth of Nations*, which was published in 1776. This visionary work advocated

The Yankee Fleet

Lighthouses were constructed along the Atlantic Coast in the eighteenth century.

Merchants and Bloody Americans Before the Revolution

The destruction of the *Gaspee* by the men of Providence, Rhode Island.

free trade, which is exactly what the colonies wanted. Adopting Smith's policies could have helped to ward off the Revolution, but by 1776, it was too late for the reactionary government of British Prime Minister Lord North and King George III to act. Like Colbert, they thought that a nation's wealth depended on a positive flow of gold into their national coffers. America's ships, with their sails filled with wind, were never intended to take trade from English vessels.

Americans were still content to ignore England and its laws regarding trade as Englishmen had done for years on both sides of the Atlantic. Namely, they would smuggle as they pleased. For a smuggler, life on the sea was not the height of comfort. Most ships tended to be wet and chilly if not downright cold. Captains and their officers could be brutal. There was little help to be had in case of illness. Most of the time, if you got sick, you died. Few career sailors lived to be forty. There was always a lot to do on a sailing ship; it was a full-time job. Even during the most horrible storms, the men had to go aloft to take in or reef the sails and engage in all sorts of dangerous activity depending on what needed to be done. Brutal mates and quartermasters, armed with a belaying pin, rope's end, cutlass, pistol or a special

The Yankee Fleet

This half crown used in the colonies was minted from Spanish silver taken in an English Naval raid on Lima in 1745. Note the word "Lima" under the head of George II, which showed the source of the silver used in the coin.

cane made of an iron rod that was covered with rings of bone and leather, did not hesitate to use their weapons along with a shod foot or a fist to make an indecisive crewman hop to it. Yet it was these men who sailed the hundreds of ships that provided an economic lifeline for the colonies.

Due to taxes like the Townshend Acts, Americans continued to engage in a lot of smuggling. In fact, being a smuggler was a fine old American practice. In an attempt to deter smuggling, the British sent armed ships, many of them fast schooners, to patrol the waters off the New England coast. Smuggling was a huge issue in England itself. For those who had believed in free trade all along, Adam Smith simply wrote it down in a coherent form. While the colonial office did not want smuggling to be a huge issue in America, it had been thus ever since the British tried to regulate trade and shipping in the 1650s. In the 1770s, the merchants and people of

Merchants and Bloody Americans Before the Revolution

The universal coin of trade in the eighteenth century, "the piece of eight."

Providence, Rhode Island, had been outraged by the very appearance of an armed British schooner, the *Gaspee*, stationed offshore, which was under orders to capture American smugglers coming out of Providence and the other area towns. It was a direct insult to hardworking New England smugglers who were working to make a living in the waters of Narragansett Bay.

The *Gaspee*'s master, a certain Lieutenant Dudingston, seemed to enjoy his job of chasing down smugglers far too much. He was an absolute zealot who proved to be too successful in the discharge of his office. The Rhode Islanders felt that he had overstepped his authority and needed to be taught a lesson and taken down a peg or two. Dudingston acted with a positive air of social superiority that earned him the undying hatred of the egalitarian Rhode Islanders. This hatred extended to his command, the *Gaspee*, as well.

The *Gaspee* was personified as the very real enemy, as well as the British revenue officials themselves, even though the vessel was an inanimate object. It wasn't even a force of nature as was the great Atlantic on which it sailed. On June 10, 1772, a packet ship left Newport on a voyage to Providence without telling Dudingston. Dudingston gave chase after the small vessel. He pursued it for twenty miles with total disregard to the safety of his command. While running before the wind at a very good clip, Dudingston ran aground on Namquit Point, which is some seven miles below Providence.

The news spread quickly from town to town all along the shore that Dudingston had gone hard aground on Namquit Point and could not be floated off again until the morning tide. The *Gaspee* was beached at an angle and could not bring its guns to bear on any potential foe. It was totally helpless. A drummer went through the streets of Providence calling the citizens to come out and attack the *Gaspee*. The delicious breeze of revolution was in the air, and the Rhode Islanders found it intoxicating.

The call to destroy the *Gaspee* was answered by a huge number of men who were told to meet at a certain Providence waterfront tavern after sunset. After a short meeting, the men embarked aboard eight large whaleboats and pushed off to attack the stranded revenue ship. It was noted that it was now half past nine o'clock in the evening. The black night skies served as a cover for the men during their attack. There was no moon, only the flickering lanterns on the *Gaspee*, seven miles to the south, guiding the assailants. The boat's oars were muffled, and not a man made a sound. The lanterns on the *Gaspee* seemed to signal to them through the darkness, as if inviting its own destruction.

At long last, the Rhode Island men covered the seven miles of open bay and silently came up to the ship at the point of land on which its captain had unwittingly left it to perish. Hardly a sound did they make as the avengers climbed aboard and fell on Captain Dudingston and his crew. The alarm aboard ship was given just as the action was all but concluded. The overpowered British crew had their hands bound behind their backs. Then they were placed like so much cordwood into the boats and set ashore unarmed and at liberty. It was a fine vantage point for Dudingston and his men to watch that which was about to happen next. As they strained to see what was going on through the darkness, flames suddenly shot up into the sky as the *Gaspee* took fire and burned.

For the Americans, it was a great sight. The fire red glow reflected on their faces and showed the exaltation that they clearly felt in this victory for unfettered commercial enterprise. In Providence, seven miles to the north, the crowd that had been keeping vigil watched as the crimson flames illuminated the night sky with mouths agape. The midnight air was rent by their cries and shouts of joy at the burning of the hated *Gaspee*. In a way it was the very first of the water fire events that would become so popular more than two hundred years later when they were introduced during the tenure of Mayor Buddy Cianci. The burning of the *Gaspee* had been a grand exploit for the men of Providence. The heroes arrived back at

Merchants and Bloody Americans Before the Revolution

A barrel wagon used on the roads of Siasconset, Nantucket, during the colonial period and through the nineteenth century to haul fish and seaweed.

Providence in the wee hours of June 11, where they were loudly cheered for their adventure in liberation. A ship of the British Royal Navy had been attacked, taken and burned by the men of the city. It was a notable triumph.

The British were not amused by the events of June 10. They even offered a huge reward of one thousand pounds sterling to anyone who would give up the names of the individuals who had burned the *Gaspee*. Not even for that princely fortune would anyone inform on the heroes of Providence. The British were beside themselves with rage. Today that reward would have a gold value of about $150,000, more or less. The British proclaimed the burning of their ship a wanton act of vandalism. Such an act was treason! And treason was an offense punishable by hanging, drawing and quartering under the British Crown, a punishment still in force in 1772. In point of fact, that is to my best knowledge, this punishment was last carried out in the British Empire some forty-three years later in upper Canada after a failed revolt in 1815. A former resident of the town of Franklin, Massachusetts, by the name of David Lane had gone north to join in the revolt against the British Crown. He was captured, found guilty of treason and hanged, drawn and quartered. I know of nobody to suffer that punishment after that time.

The Yankee Fleet

I often wonder if Mr. Lane would rather have declined this honor of being among the last to suffer this ancient ritual.

In 1770, the Boston Massacre took place, and the Boston Tea Party followed in December of 1773. This was in turn followed by the passage of the punitive Intolerable Acts of 1774, which closed the port of Boston and thereby killed the city's trade and thus its economy. The Quartering Act also punished the city by forcing the colonists to house the occupying British troops. Almost all the trouble leading up to the break with England had something to do with maritime commerce. Outrage piled on outrage until the Continental Congress met in two sessions in Philadelphia in 1774 and 1775, formed an army and subsequently drove the British from American soil by April of 1776. By July 4 of that year, the United States declared independence from England and its restrictive trade policies. The war on land and on the sea was just about to begin.

Chapter 6

THE SAILING NAVY AT WAR

When the American Revolution began, there was no United States Navy. Washington organized a small fleet of scouting vessels, and this proved to be a beginning. Of all the ships remembered from the Revolutionary War, the best remembered was the ship that sank in its first engagement under the flag of the new nation. It was a gift from France, an old French frigate, long past its prime called *Le Bonhomme Richard* in tribute to Boston-born Ben Franklin. As stated, Washington had called for a flotilla of schooners to operate in many capacities as his water-going eyes and ears, as messengers, and as a limited combat naval force. During the war, some new warships were built, like the *Ranger* and the *Alfred*, but the most well-known ship of the period was that ancient French frigate given to the United States to be used as a commerce raider. The French government had a great fondness for America's representative to Versailles, Benjamin Franklin. And it was for that reason, they wished their old vessel renamed in his honor.

Le Bonhomme Richard loosely translates to *Poor Richard* which was an obvious homage to Franklin's famous *Poor Richard's Almanac*. It seems that this little book was favored by the philosophers of the Enlightenment. Franklin's ship was not only an old frigate far past its prime, but it was also over gunned. That is to say it carried too much firepower. This might not be a problem on most later iron and steel ships, but on a wooden sailing ship of war, it could be fatal. Firing too many cannon could open the seams of an elderly wooden ship. *Le Bonhomme Richard* was sailing on borrowed time. It would be almost sound just as long as it didn't have to fire too many guns in the heat of battle.

And speaking of guns, the cannon on the ship were very old and also stressed by time and overuse. Although cannon hadn't changed very much in their fundamental technology over the last century or so, they were expensive to make and were therefore recycled. Captured guns were highly prized and were found all over the European military establishments. They were like travelers who had really been around. Too many of *Bonhomme Richard*'s cannon had very little time left in them

Early copperplate print of John Paul Jones struck after his victory over the British *Serapis*.

before they would explode under the stress imposed by metal fatigue. They had just experienced too active a service life, some for over a century, as had the ship. *Bonhomme Richard* and its cannon were long overdue at the ship breaker's yard and the melting pots of cannon foundries.

A Scot by the name of John Paul Jones, who would prove to be something of a naval genius sought throughout his later lifetime by everybody including Catherine the Great, was named commander of this imposing, three-masted dinosaur of considerable size, which should never fire its guns in anger or even in minor agitation. This ship attracted many New Englanders to its crew who had a lot of practical sailing experience and a lot of resentment for the English, in equal parts, because of British interference in trade and their profession. Most Massachusetts seamen had been angry with the English since the port of Boston had been closed in 1774. For the Yankees, it was high time for payback.

Jones saw his role as that of a commerce raider. He even treated some English coastal towns to a bit of cannonading. King George III and his government saw this as very cheeky indeed, and they declared that Jones was a traitor having been born in the British Isles on the Firth of Fourth in Scotland. Jones was having none of it and went on bringing the war home to merry old England. Many a Yankee boy on Jones's ship rejoiced at the former mother country's distress. In 1779, Jones and the ship *Alfred* spied a convoy of fifty English merchantmen under the protection of the Royal Navy's HMS *Countess of Scarborough* and HMS *Serapis*. *Alfred* engaged the *Countess of Scarborough* and Jones took on the larger and better armed HMS *Serapis*.

Bonhomme Richard opened the proceedings with a broadside. Several of the cannon exploded killing their gun crews. After a short while, the ship's seams began to open to the waters of the Atlantic. Yet, the ships went on exchanging fire for about two hours. Almost as many of Jones's men were killed by their military equipment as by the English cannon fire and falling spars not to mention splinters of wood. It was rumored that during the heat of battle, Jones actually shot an American sailor who tried to surrender the ship on his own by attempting to lower the flag. I do not think that the story was anything more than an embellishment, but who can tell for certain. Jones was possessed of that sort of grim determination. Maybe he did shoot the man. He was a testy Scot after all.

After two hours of slaughter, *Bonhomme Richard*'s decks ran red with American blood. And to top it off, the ship appeared to be sinking. Most likely because it was sinking! At that point in the battle, the commander of HMS *Serapis* is reputed to have given Jones the chance to surrender. I rather think the discussion might have gone on like this, "I say Jones, your ship appears to be sinking. Too bad that. Care to surrender?"

I can just close my eyes and hear Jones calling out in his distinctive burr, "Toffey-nosed so-and-so." And then he must have said in a louder voice, "I hae naught yet begun tah fite."

The Yankee Fleet

Early print of the battle between *Le Bonhomme Richard* and HMS *Serapis*.

Then the Englishman might have hollered back, "Sorry Jones, couldn't make anything out of that. Could you please repeat that? Now there's a good chap!"

Jones would holler back at the top of his booming and commanding Scot's voice, "I hae naught yet begun tah fite ye twit. Are ye deaf or just too damn stupid tah understand the concept!!!"

But whatever historic exchange might have taken place, one thing was for sure, and that was that Jones's ship was sinking. However, he was not inclined to surrender to the British and be brought back to England to be hanged or worse. He brought his ship close to the *Serapis*, threw grappling hooks onto it and hauled the ship in closer so that he could board it. When the gap between the two ships had narrowed enough, he leaped aboard with his uninjured crew. They had real inspiration to fight like the devil. Their ship was sinking!

The fighting was fierce, and no quarter was given by the Americans. Jones was a desperate man. At last, the British were contained and forced to surrender. Their captain was wounded, and his crew was spent in the face of the savage Yankee onslaught. The victory was played up back home as the greatest American naval achievement to date. And it was. The British navy had eggs on its face this time. A ship of the Royal Navy had been soundly defeated by Americans! And they were licked by an American ship that was sinking at that!

The Sailing Navy at War

Following the Revolution, the navy, such as it was, was abandoned. Under the Articles of Confederation, the government had no authority to tax. There was no money to support the navy. Even after the Constitution went into effect in 1789, there was still no provision made for a navy. Until the Revolution, the Barbary pirates of North Africa had not attacked American shipping because the colonies were under the protection of the British fleet, which included six hundred warships of various sizes ranging from ten-gun sloops of war to the ships of the line each carrying seventy-five to one hundred guns and crews and marines to the number of a thousand men.

The Barbary pirates did not attempt to interfere with British shipping. The British were known to exact awful revenge on those who harassed their citizens anywhere on the globe. In one instance, a British shop was sacked in the Turkish Empire, and the British fleet appeared sometime later to exact terrible retribution. They shelled the city as an object lesson. It was in the tradition of the Roman Empire at its height. If a Roman citizen in any part of the Roman world was attacked, the whole military might of the state would come down on the offending party. One had only to say, "I'm British," to be safe in many parts of the eighteenth-century world. Americans had lost that right with independence. They were no longer British, nor did they have the protection that went with being British. The Barbary pirates now saw American ships and their cargo as fair game.

The Barbary pirates wasted no time in taking American prizes and selling their cargoes and people for a fine profit. When the Washington government came to power in 1789, envoys to the pirate states worked out deals that would cost the U.S. a million dollars or more a year to buy off the Barbary pirates with tributes, and in some cases, with fine American ships. These tribute ships were always built smaller than their usual tonnage and comparable American vessels. Without warships, there was little more that the government of the United States could do. Books were published like *Robin's Journal*, which told tales of Americans sold into slavery by North African pirates. It was not until 1794 that real thought was given to the founding of a proper navy. The cause of this development was the Napoleonic Wars, which featured a contest for power in Europe between France, and its changing allies, and Britain, and its changing allies, lasting from 1789 to 1815 with a few "time outs" here and there. In 1794 Congress at long last authorized the construction of six frigates.

Washington had issued the Proclamation of Neutrality in 1793 in an effort to keep the United States out of war with either France or Britain. France had begun to pressure the United States to honor the treaty of alliance that Franklin had negotiated back in 1778. The United States argued that the alliance no longer held because it was negotiated with the government of Louis XVI, and the French Republicans had chopped his head off and changed the government. As far as Washington was concerned that ended the treaty. The French didn't see it that way, and the United States ended up in an undeclared naval war with France from 1798 to 1800.

The Yankee Fleet

The view from Fort Adams at Newport, Rhode Island, circa 1875.

New England shipping found itself under French attack at sea. The British were also taking U.S. ships bound on commercial voyages to France. But that became a minor issue as the principal problem was with the French. Lord Nelson, the great hero of the naval war against France, did the United States a great service when he sank or captured all but two small French warships during the Battle of the Nile in Egypt in 1798.

Now, let us consider exactly what constitutes a frigate. A frigate was a two-decked warship of 175 to 200 hundred feet in length mounting thirty-six to forty-four guns. Frigates had three masts and carried crews of 275 to 400 men. English frigates of the period were 160 to 180 feet in length, and they most often mounted thirty-six or thirty-eight guns. The American ships were to be of much heavier construction than their British counterparts and about 200 or more feet in length. The greater length and weight of the American ships resulted in a problem called "hogging." Hogging occurred when a ship exceeded the normal length for its framing. If the ship was like the *Constitution*, Boston's very own celebrity warship, the two ends—the bow and the stern—would tend to pull downward making the ship bow in the center because of its overall length of 208 feet.

The problem was solved by the use of great diagonal crossbeams to brace the midship and prevent the sagging of the bow and stern. These innovations gave huge strength and stability to the American ships making them the finest in the world of their class and ensuring that the *Constitution* and its counterparts were much stronger than any British frigate. The *Constitution* was built of live oak and its sides were two feet thick. It mounted forty-four cannons and threw a much heavier broadside than could any French or British ship of its class. Only a ship of the line could stand up to the *Constitution*. But this ship would not make its mark in the undeclared war with France. France's problems were so great that by 1800, First Consul Napoleon Bonaparte ordered his foreign minister, Talleyrand, to conclude a peace treaty with

The Sailing Navy at War

Decatur burning the *Philadelphia*. From an old engraving.

the United States. Talleyrand was well known in the United States. He had left France one step ahead of the executioner of Paris during the days of the Reign of Terror, and he summered in New York with Aaron Burr at Richmond Hill and with Phillip Schyler at his home in Albany, as well as in Massachusetts with a British planter who had a summer home in the town of Wrentham on Lake Archer. Now he was forced to deal with the Americans who had refused him a bribe in the notorious XYZ Affair almost three years before. President John Adams had shown great leadership during this period by arming for a war but not actively engaging in one. He even called Washington to service and put him at the head of all of the armed forces and militias. All fighting with the French was on the high seas in the form of commerce raiding.

Jefferson was the first leader to face off openly against a foreign enemy, the Barbary pirates. They took their annual tribute and attacked U.S. shipping too. During the early nineteenth century, it was not strange to hear the names of Yankees read out in New England churches as people captured by Barbary pirates. Like so many casualties of war, they were publicly remembered. Many a Massachusetts man lingered in a cell or in bondage in Tunis, Morocco, Tripoli or Algiers in 1801. Some Yankee women even found themselves in situations for which their Puritan upbringing had ill prepared them. Americans were getting angry over the bad faith shown by the North African pirate city-states of the Barbary Coast. But the United State had warships now. Among them were the super frigates *Constitution, President, United States, Constellation* and *Philadelphia*. The nation had other lesser ships as well, and President Jefferson thought that the ships should show the flag in the Mediterranean Sea.

Thousands of Yankees and other Americans were being held for ransom, and millions of dollars were being paid out to get these poor souls released from captivity. Jefferson sent four warships to the Mediterranean to enforce the treaties made with the various North African pirate sultans. The *Philadelphia* was one of the best among them. It was captained by one of the most talented men in the navy, Captain Bainbridge, but even the best of men can make mistakes. Captain Bainbridge, who was to gain fame in the War of 1812 as a commander of other vessels, made the mistake of giving chase to a smaller Tripolitan ship in strange waters that the navy had not yet charted. As a result, he ran the *Philadelphia* hard aground with its guns too elevated on one side of the ship and too low on the other to bring them to bear on an enemy. The ship was quickly surrounded by the sons of the prophet and was captured.

The *Philadelphia* was one of the most powerful ships in the Mediterranean and was now the largest in the Tripolitan pirate fleet. There was no way that this situation could be allowed to stand. The question was what to do. Could the ship be recaptured now that the Tripolitans had floated her? A young navy lieutenant by the name of Stephen Decatur proposed attacking the ship under the cover of night with the purpose of either recapturing it or setting the *Philadelphia* on fire if recapture was not a possibility. With a crew of volunteers, he set out on this dangerous mission. With his men aboard a small, captured Tripolitan ship, he approached the *Philadelphia* as if to anchor for the night. It was a clever ruse, which worked admirably well. Once the Americans had arrived at their destination, they quietly made their way up the sides of the big ship. They fell on the Muslim crew, which had been stationed aboard *Philadelphia,* and recaptured the vessel in less than ten minutes of vicious fighting.

Decatur did attempt a rescue of the big ship, but it was just impossible to get the *Philadelphia* under way in the short grace period that the battle had bought them. Decatur then gave the order to set fire to the magnificent vessel. As the Americans pulled away, it was a bittersweet moment. They had achieved a great goal in keeping the *Philadelphia* out of the pirate's hands, but the loss of that ship was a heavy one. Bainbridge was brought very low in spirit by its loss. Commodore Edward Preble, commander of the squadron, held a meeting on his flagship the USS *Constitution*. He decided to blockade Tripoli until the ruler of that stronghold could see the error of his piratical ways and policies. With the big American frigates outside of the Harbor of Tripoli, commercial life in the city came to a halt. Tripoli was now starving for

The Sailing Navy at War

commerce. The American squadron's few but very large and powerful ships had no trouble dominating the smaller Barbary vessels even though they were far more numerous. Tripoli fell into line and agreed to live up to its treaty with the United States. The date was February 15, 1804. One by one Tunis, Algiers and Morocco saw the light as well.

Eleven years later, the *Constitution* would return to the Barbary city-states as flagship of the most powerful fleet ever to sail under the flag of the United States. One by one the harbors and shipping of the Barbary city-states would be destroyed in a fierce bombardment of solid shot and mortars rented from the king of the Two Sicilies. The rulers of those pirate states were told that the government of the United States would never again pay tribute to them, and if any American ship was to be attacked in the future, there would be hell to pay when an even more powerful force returned. After this little visit by the American fleet, there would be no more problems with the Barbary pirates. American commercial shipping could spread its sails in perfect safety from the North African pirates who were put out of business by the French in 1830 when they seized the whole area of what became the Department of Algeria. An American squadron remained on station in the Mediterranean to make sure that the sons of the prophet and others behaved themselves.

Isaiah Thomas's *Farmers Almanac* of 1807 reported that the United States navy included twenty-four warships that mounted 574 guns and had the manpower of 66,000 seamen. Not all of these men served on the ships. Some were in support vessels, stationed in forts, stationed on naval bases, in dockyards and in dry docks. The makeup of these crews was international. Even as late as 1898, the USS *Maine* had a crew composed of individuals from more than four dozen political entities. It was not so very different in 1807. In this time period, Great Britain was fighting for its life with France who dominated most of Europe.

England's stress led the country to employ something called Orders in Council, which translates to impressment. Impressment was a fine old British naval custom by which the Royal Navy kept up the number of seamen servicing its six hundred plus ships. Most of the time a press gang, led by an officer, would surround a waterfront tavern and then enter it. They would then proceed to take as many men as they needed to serve on the ship or ships from which they came. The only thing that would save a man from the press gang was if that man could prove that he was a "gentleman." His inability to do so would result in his impressment. One of the reasons one or two officers would go along on the forced recruiting venture was that it was possible for them to recognize a gentleman if they saw one.

On the high seas, things were a bit different. British ships would randomly stop vessels that could not defend themselves, board them, muster their crews and detect "deserters from the Royal Navy," and then force them back to duty. Were there deserters from the Royal Navy on American ships? Yes, there were. The British navy was a horrible place to serve. The food was bloody awful, and the discipline worse. Floggings were rampant for the smallest infractions. If a jack-tar did the big

The Yankee Fleet

Captain Lawrence of the USS *Chesapeake*.

one, that is strike an officer, he could be flogged by the entire fleet. In this process, the condemned was trussed up in a standing position in a boat, stripped to the waist and rowed to every ship in the fleet. The ship's crew would be mustered to witness the punishment. The petty officer in charge would flog the man on his naked back fifty times with a cat-o'-nine-tails. The "cat" was a brutal whip with nine individual braided leather pieces, which sometimes had an encased bit of lead at the end of each strand. Fifty strokes would lift 450 pieces of flesh from the flogged man's back at each ship in the fleet mustered to witness the punishment.

Men would not survive this treatment. Halfway around the fleet, naked and bleeding spines and ribs were exposed and were all that was left of the man's back to be flogged. Yet the punishment had to be observed by all ships left in the fleet. In 1707, for attempting to tell an admiral by the name of Shovel that he and his fleet were indeed off course, a seaman was hanged from the yardarm for offering such an opinion. Shortly thereafter the entire British squadron piled up on the Isle of Scilley and was lost. Such was service in the eighteenth- and early nineteenth-century British navy. Men deserted wholesale whenever the chance presented itself. No independent New Englander would ever survive in such a place. There were two mutinies in the British fleets in the late 1790s that led to some small reforms, but life was strictly *Billy Budd* as in Melville's novel. Also it must be remembered that service in the navy was for the course of a conflict, not for a fixed number of years. War between England and France was to go on for more than twenty-five years with a few breaks here and there from 1789 to 1815.

It was intolerable to Americans that British warships would stop merchant ships that flew the flag of the United States to impress sailors into their service. It was entirely possible that there were British nationals working on American ships. It was also true that there were British deserters on American ships. But that was not the point. Even in Boston, which was a major trading partner with England, there was a great deal of resentment over the issue of impressment.

It became an issue of American pride in 1807 when the British man-of-war HMS *Leopard* came upon the smaller American warship *Chesapeake* and demanded that a press gang be allowed to come aboard the American warship. Captain James Lawrence refused the British request. One has to remember that a ship just didn't start firing guns at the drop of a hat. A ship had to be cleared for battle. Buckets of water had to be placed near each gun in case of fire. The gun decks had to be sanded for safety's sake. The sailors had to get rid of their shoes so that they would not slip in the inevitable blood. If there was furniture in the cabins, which were almost always gun decks too, it had to be put in nets and hauled up the mast or stowed deep in the ship out of the way. On some ships, the captain's furniture was even thrown overboard, which must have given some satisfaction to unhappy sailors. Under the circumstances of battle, they could get away with it too.

Lawrence decided to fight in spite of the fact that the ship was half an hour away from being cleared for action. The British attacked with a broadside, and for twenty minutes the well-prepared larger vessel punished the *Chesapeake*. Lawrence was fatally wounded at the start of the action, and as he lay near death, he issued his famous order, "Don't give up the ship."

The Americans had no choice but to surrender even as they had been battered within sight of Fortress Monroe. The British boarded *Chesapeake* and removed four sailors who had survived the battle in which the American vessel had hardly fired a shot. Of the four men taken to the *Leopard*, one was hanged for desertion from the British navy as an object lesson. The result of this incident was that President Jefferson and Congress put the Embargo Act into effect. This act ended trade with England much to the anger of New Englanders whose lifeblood depended on trade with Britain. Smuggling became rampant in New England and the other states. Newspapers published cartoons of smugglers being bitten in their nether quarters by a creature called an Ograbme that had the appearance of an alligator. Of course "Ograbme" was embargo spelled backward. After Jefferson left office, the embargo was lifted and open trade with England was resumed.

Sailors were still being impressed, but a little payback was in the offing. The USS *President* happened on HMS *Little Belt* sailing off the United States coast looking for sailors to impress. This time it was the American warship that was fully cleared for action. The United States man-of-war fell on the unhappy *Little Belt* and pounded it to sawdust. By 1812, Congress—led by Henry Clay, who also led the War Hawks, a faction of Congress that was spoiling for a war with Britain—declared war against England. The ironic thing was that the very day that war was declared by the United States, England revoked the Orders in Council, which was the cause of all the trouble in the first place. The War of 1812 was totally unneeded and would result in needless deaths, loss of shipping, the burning of Washington and the harming of trade to the point that the New England states hosted the Hartford Convention and almost broke away from the union.

Most of the good war news, in those dark days, was the result of exploits by the Boston-built USS *Constitution*, a beautiful frigate with forty-four guns. It was said that the ship could fight any two British frigates or even a ship of the line with seventy-four guns. The *Constitution* was designed by Joshua Humphries and built in Boston of live oak. Its sides were planked with two feet of oak, and it was sheathed with copper-plates made by Paul Revere. The ship's first duty was coastal patrol in 1798. The *Constitution* was, and still is, a beautiful ship and the pride of its home port, Boston, Massachusetts.

Later the ship made a name for itself as flagship of the Mediterranean squadron under the command of Commodore Preble as mentioned previously. In 1807, it returned for a two-year refitting out, and in 1809, it was made the flagship of the Atlantic squadron then under the command of Commodore John Rogers. Captain Isaac Hull was its commander in 1812. It was during this time that the USS *Constitution* had one of its greatest adventures, and it didn't include the firing of even a single cannon. Shortly after the declaration of war, the *Constitution* sailed out of Boston

The Sailing Navy at War

The U.S. government issued a stamp in 1947 honoring the 150th anniversary of the launching of the USS *Constitution* featuring the original Humphries's drawing of the famed frigate.

Harbor. It was very important to the nation that one of its most powerful ships not be caught in a blockade situation and kept out of action against the British.

Hull headed the ship out to sea. Not long after, the *Constitution* was sighted off the coast of New Jersey by five British warships. The *Constitution* could have fought any of them individually, but all five at once was too great a challenge for any ship. It was very fast and had just been refitted, but there was only one problem. The wind died. A sailing ship depends on the wind for propulsion. Hull was not about to lose his ship without using every device at his command to save it. He ordered the sails wet down so that every bit of wind could be caught. Then he ordered the ship's boats to row in advance of the ship with the big kedge anchors. These anchors were dropped, and the sailors then bent their backs to take the anchors up again. This moved the ship slowly forward away from danger.

Seeing what the Americans were up to, the British followed suit, and their ships moved after the American frigate. Hull continued to edge forward and stayed far enough ahead of the British as to remain out of range of their powerful "ship breaker" guns, which were short and fired a very powerful, heavy load. Slowly the distance between the opposing forces grew greater, and by the time Egg Harbor, New Jersey, was sighted the *Constitution* had managed its escape. This was on July 17, 1812. The *Constitution* would live to fight another day.

And as it was, that day was not long in coming. In August, just about one month later, the *Constitution* met **HMS** *Guerriere* while cruising the Atlantic waters. The big

Captain Isaac Hull.

American ship cleared for action and bore down on the British frigate. British and French frigates were slightly smaller and less heavily built and armed than American ships of that class. The *Constitution's* forty-four guns would be answered by thirty-eight on the British ship, which had originally been built by the French and then captured and refitted out by England. The battle lasted but twenty minutes before the Americans turned *Guerriere* into matchwood without masts. The British would later claim that the Americans were taking unfair advantage of them because the Americans had overbuilt their ships. The people of Boston and the nation cheered over the victory of their pet warship. Their favorite story of the great battle and defeat of the much-hated British was spread around the Charlestown Navy Yard, waterfront taverns, marketplace and then the whole city of old Boston itself. That story, which was quite true, was that when the *Guerriere* opened fire on the *Constitution*, some of its shot bounced off the very thick sides of the American ship. After the battle, the sailors began calling their vessel "Old Ironsides." The name has stuck to this very day.

In December of 1812, *Constitution* spied another British frigate in the offering and fell upon it. That British warship was the *Java*. This time there would be no twenty-minute battle. For three hours the ships maneuvered for position and exchanged broadsides with deadly effect. At the conclusion of the battle, *Java's* masts were shot away and a large portion of its crew was killed or wounded. The British surrendered the ship. Orders went out from the first sea lord that British frigates were not to seek engagements with American frigates on a one-on-one basis. The great superiority of the American ships was clearly recognized. During the rest of the War of 1812, the Americans had a difficult time in finding targets for their guns on anything like an equal footing. *Constitution* chased many of the British navy ships and added eight of them to its bag, including a brace in one engagement in which it captured two British men-of-war at one time. Considering how badly the war had gone on land, the war on the water was going well indeed.

One of Massachusetts's better-known privateers of the War of 1812 was Captain Joseph Babson. He was the son of a most distinguished Gloucester family who was born to Captain and Mrs. William Babson on June 2, 1777. Captain William Babson had also been a privateer who was lost during the Revolutionary War on his ship the *Gloucester* in 1777; he never got a chance to know his son. Joseph grew to manhood and went to sea. In short order, he also became a captain and made many successful commercial voyages. Some of these were of two-year duration. When the War of 1812 began against England, Captain Joseph Babson fitted out a ship and became a privateer like his father, to whom he felt a special connection despite the fact that he had never known him. During the next two years, he took prizes on the high seas, making a reputation for himself. It was about this time that he was painted by one of the most prolific portrait artists of the period, Michel Felice Corne.

Corne was born on the island of Elba, most famed for being the place of Napoleon's first exile, in 1752. He migrated to America and settled in the small but

The Yankee Fleet

The navy yard at Kittery, Maine.

cosmopolitan town of Newport, Rhode Island. Here he became one of the most celebrated portrait artists of the day. He had studied in Leghorn, Italy, where he mastered his strong naturalistic style. Corne also worked in Salem and Newport, as well as Boston. He died at Newport in 1845 at the ripe old age of ninety-three.

Babson's strength is reflected in Corne's portrait. Babson distinguished himself as the master of the *Orlando* during the war. He was both a patriot and made it pay "right well" by taking many rich prizes. His family prospered, and in time, he took as his wife his second cousin, Polly Babson. The most accomplished of their children was Daniel Tarr Babson, a great friend of artist Fitz Hugh Lane who painted a double portrait of Daniel and his wife about 1863. Captain Joseph Babson died on April 2, 1839, in his sixty-third year. He was a typical man of his class and time who earned his living on the sea. Considering the rough nature of life on the ocean under the snap of the wind in the sails, he was lucky to have lived so long and to have died in comparative comfort.

To be quite candid, the War of 1812 was actually a sideshow for the British who were fighting Napoleon and his allies for the life of the empire itself as the main attraction. Although Napoleon was spawned by the French Revolution, he was the very essence of despotism, and England was the closest thing to a democracy in Europe. But the American war was costly from every aspect. The British had lost important naval contests on Lake Erie to Commodore Oliver Hazard Perry and on Lake Champlain to Commodore Thomas MacDonough. On December 24, 1814, the Treaty of Ghent was signed by John Quincy Adams, Albert Gallatin and the great War Hawk himself, Henry Clay, for the United States and Lord Gambier for Britain. The war ended with the conclusion that everything would

The Sailing Navy at War

Captain Joseph Babson, who followed in his father's footsteps by becoming a highly successful privateer, is pictured in this painting by Michel Corne.

The *Constitution* during its 1830s refit.

return to the existing state of affairs prewar. The question of impressment was never addressed.

What Gambier failed to tell Adams was that General Sir Edward Packenham was with a large British fleet sailing to Louisiana to take New Orleans. Gambier's thinking was that nothing could be done about the situation now, and that a British victory might lead to some useful spoils. On January 8, 1815, General Andrew Jackson with the help of pirate Jean LaFitte, smashed Packenham's army costing the English the loss of 30 percent of their forces, their commanding officer and their pride. The soldiers who had defeated Napoleon in Europe were smashed by backwoodsmen, militia forces and a smattering of pirates even though they outnumbered the Americans greatly. America's ironmen and wooden ships had combined to win a great moral victory in the war that never should have been fought in the first place.

After the War of 1812, the *Constitution* was enshrined in the hearts and literature of the American people and is our oldest commissioned warship. The ship even survived plans for scrapping, and it survived some pretty bad reconstructions, as well as some great indignities. The famed frigate had undergone an impressive refitting in the mid-1830s. Among other embellishments, when it returned to active service in 1835, it had received a new figurehead of President Andrew Jackson himself, the hero of New Orleans! This didn't sit well with the anti-Jackson New England crowd who had met at the Hartford Convention to oppose the war and even discussed quitting the union.

The new Jackson figurehead outraged Boston to the degree that the *Constitution* was actually moved out of the Charlestown Navy Yard and anchored at its traditional offshore station with one navy vessel guarding its port side and another on the starboard side. When Jackson's head was being carved for the front of the ship, the carver was so harassed that the half-carved block was removed to the navy yard for the finishing of the work under marine guard. But as the ship rested at anchor one dark night, a young Cape Cod sea captain by the name of Samuel Dewey rowed out to the ship with muffled oars. On the night Dewey chose for his adventure, a severe rainstorm raged with thunder and lightning. The captain rowed under the figurehead, moored his boat and climbed up onto Jackson's figure. He then proceeded to saw off Jackson's head.

A group of Dewey's friends gathered at Gallagher's Hotel in Boston to throw him a party. About this time, Commodore J.D. Elliot, the commander who had felt himself the protector of his chief's sacred effigy, was in a frantic rage over this affront to Jackson's dignity. Dewey was not afraid to court danger. In fact, he went to Washington to face Jackson in person with his trophy. On arriving in the capital, Dewey went over to the Department of the Navy to confront Mahlon Dickerson, the secretary of the navy himself. The short, chunky sailor badgered Dickerson's secretary into allowing him access to Dickerson. On entering the navy secretary's office, Dewey said, "Have I the honor of addressing the secretary of the navy?"

"You have," replied Dickerson, "And, as I am very busy, I will thank you to be brief."

"Mr. Dickerson," said the Captain, "I am the man who removed the figurehead from the *Constitution*, and I have brought it here to restore it."

"Well sir, you are the man who had the audacity to disfigure *Old Ironsides*?"

Dewey responded, "Yes sir. I took the responsibility."

The secretary of the navy yelled, "Well sir, I'll have you arrested immediately," and he began to ring his bell.

Dewey said, "Stop Mr. Secretary. You as a lawyer know that there is no statute against defacing a ship of war, and all you can do is sue me for trespassing and that in the county where the offense was committed. If you desire it, I will go back to Middlesex County in Massachusetts where the crime was committed and stand trial there."

Dickerson thought for a moment then said, "You are right, and now tell me how you took away the head."

Dewey told his story from beginning to end. Dickerson then asked Dewey to remain while he went over to the White House followed by a messenger who carried the head still in the cloth that Dewey had wrapped around it. When Jackson heard

The Yankee Fleet

Captain Dewey presents President Jackson's head to Secretary of the Navy Dickerson.

the story and saw the head, he burst into laughter. "Why that," he laughed, "why that is the most infernal graven image I ever saw. The fellow did perfectly right. You've got him you say; well give him a kick and my compliments, and tell him to saw it off again."

It is interesting to note that during the refitting of the *Constitution* a lot of its original material was replaced, and some of the oak was made into a carriage built especially for Jackson. And that carriage took Jackson and Van Buren to Van Buren's inauguration on March 4, 1837. Dewey went often to Washington after that, and was eventually named to the position of postmaster in Virginia. On his visiting card, he had his name and address on one side and a depiction of a handsaw on the other. On the handsaw was the name Dewey and under the saw were the words, "I came, I saw, I conquered."

Old Ironsides is still with us after many restorations in Charlestown, Massachusetts. And there you can visit the ship. The rest of the sailing navy is gone. Steam was the beginning of the end. Fulton's *Clermont*, which was not the first steamboat but the first practical steamboat, made history in 1807 with its sail down the Hudson River at an impressive speed of four miles an hour. In 1817, the *Savannah* became the first vessel to cross the Atlantic partially under steam. Steam was dirty, but the handwriting was on the wall. During the next century, steam would all but replace sail, but in 1817, sail still had a good run before it. As far as the sailing navy was concerned, its days were more closely numbered, as were the wooden ships they powered in the great fleets of the world.

The last really great wooden warship to be entirely powered by sail was the 350-foot-long *Pennsylvania*. Its keel was laid down in 1818 as the world's greatest ship of the line. It was a three-decked vessel and the most expensive ship of its kind ever to be constructed. In fact it cost so much money that Congress built the *Pennsylvania* in fits and starts. Only so much money was appropriated each year for its construction. It took almost twenty years to finish the ship. By then it was already a dinosaur. The *Pennsylvania* was even larger than the *Agamemnon*, which helped to lay Cyrus Field's first Atlantic cable in 1858.

In 1861, at the start of the Civil War, the *Pennsylvania* was at the naval shipyard and base at Newport News, Virginia. It was there with a large element of the United States Atlantic fleet along with the powerful steamship of war, USS *Merrimack*. The officer in charge of the shipyard had no idea about what was to be done with the capital vessels in his charge. The whole United States Navy numbered only thirty-six ships fit for duty. The man in charge of the Newport News shipyard dithered, and then he got drunk instead of getting the ships out to the safety of the Atlantic. President Buchanan's cabinet was as worthless as he was, and his major ambition was to turn his office over to Lincoln before war broke out between the North and South. In the end, as the Confederate forces closed in on the Newport News navy yard it was decided that all the ships that could not get out to sea should be burned, which was almost all of them.

The Yankee Fleet

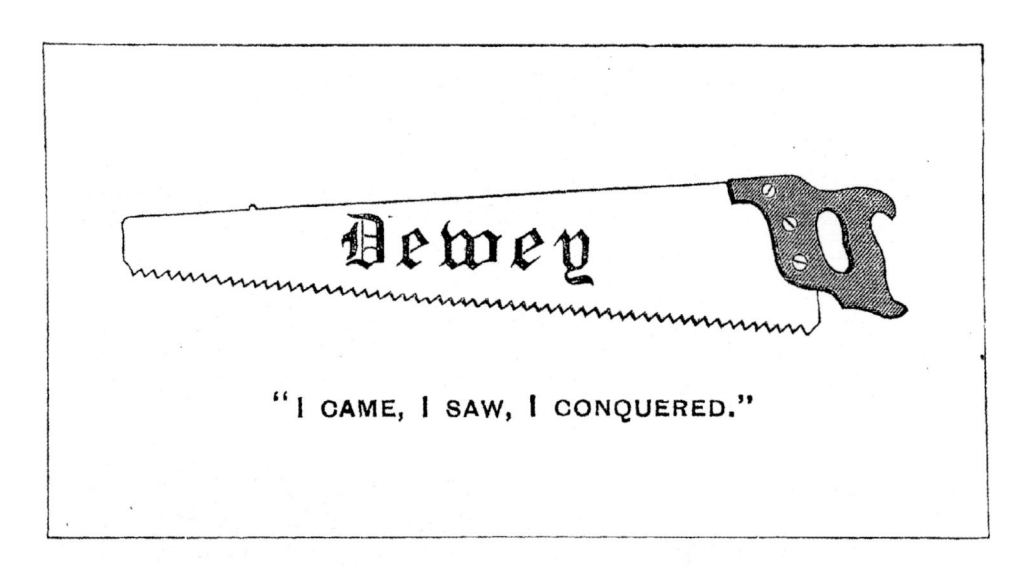

Captain Dewey's calling card.

The Gigantic ship of the line *Pennsylvania*, which was burned when the Norfolk navy yard was abandoned in 1861.

The Sailing Navy at War

The ironclads USS *Monitor* and CSS *Virginia* in the 1862 battle at Hampton Roads, which ended the domination of wooden fighting ships worldwide.

Without ever having fired a shot in anger, the *Pennsylvania* was burned. A decade and a half before, ships participating in the Mexican War had been powered by steam, as were most of the Union vessels of the Civil War, and as were the vessels involved in monumental missions like Commodore M.C. Perry's mission to Japan in 1853 and 1854. After the 1862 battle between the USS *Monitor* and the rebuilt *Merrimack*, renamed the CSS *Virginia*, wooden warships were things of the past. In the 1850s, the British ironclad HMS *Warrior* and France's *La Glorie* had ended the wooden warship as a weapon of serious consideration by any important naval power. Apart from any other factor, iron ships were lighter and stronger than wooden ones. And steel ships were to be even lighter and stronger. The day of the wooden ship of the line, frigate and sloop of war was over.

Chapter 7

Eight Hundred Brave Americans A-whaling for to Go

Herman Melville's great work *Moby Dick* is really two books. One of them is a compelling novel, and the other is a sort of textbook on whaling that leans heavily on the scientific mind of Georges Cuvier and the practical experiences of Melville himself. To understand Melville and the complex personalities in his book is to understand whaling itself. Whaling began in Massachusetts as a shore-based industry. The Native Americans began taking the right whales off shore, and the Europeans followed them, hunting the whales in the same way. Unlike the Native Americans, the British colonists were not interested in the whale primarily as food source, but rather as an economic resource. Whales were a source of highly marketable oil used both for lighting and for the lubrication of machinery.

The British colonists of Plymouth and Massachusetts Bay built towers on land rises along the shore. The colonists climbed into these and scanned the sea for whales. When a whale was sighted, the lookout called out to the company of whalers to turn out, get to their boats and row after the behemoths. Since whales often stay submerged for twenty minutes or so, when they come up, or breach, they release the exhausted air from their lungs through their spouts. The whale actually expels steamy exhaust from his lungs made up of carbon dioxide vapor as do all mammals, including man. Hence the whaler's cry of, "There she breaches. There she blows!" as an indication that a whale has been sighted because of the plume-like geyser issuing from the aperture on top of its head.

The whalers would climb into their boats and quietly row as close to the whale as they could. The harpooner would then throw or thrust his harpoon deeply into the whale. The boat would be quickly backed off so that the whale, who naturally objected to such sharp treatment, would not smash the boat with its flukes, tail or any other part of its body. The head of the harpoon would be so articulated on its steel shaft that when it turned it would fix itself in the whale's muscular tissues so that it could not be drawn out of the flesh. In point of fact, many recovered harpoon steel shafts look like corkscrews. Some old whales, when captured, had several harpoons

The Yankee Fleet

Taking a sperm whale about 1845.

embedded in their flesh, which they had accumulated over a long life at sea. There are even records of captains and mates retrieving harpoons that they had lost in fights with whales from the same beasts many years later and thousands of miles from where they had first struck them. These old harpoons would become twisted into the whales' muscles when the huge beasts responded to the irritation of the harpoon. The steel shaft holding the toggled point was attached to a wooden handle of four and a half to six feet in length. A very long rope would be attached to the harpoon. The rope was almost a half-mile long and was coiled in a large tub at the bow of the boat.

The rope, which was attached to the harpoon, would exit the boat through a notch in the bow of the craft at such a high speed that the front oarsman would have to stand over it with a bucket pouring water on it to cool the line and the notched area of the bow; otherwise, a fire might start from the immense friction of the speeding hemp against the wood. All aboard had to keep clear of the rope, for if the rope got coiled around a stray limb, that arm or leg would be cut off and pulled by the rope through the notch by a thirty- to fifty-ton whale dragging the boat over the waves at a high rate of speed. This flying trip over the blue deep became known as a Nantucket sleigh ride. The boat was commanded by the sailor responsible for steering, most often a ship's officer or sometimes the captain himself. As Captain Ahab says in *Moby Dick*, "As there is but one God in Heaven, there is but one captain aboard this ship."

On a sailing ship, just as on any ship, the captain was a law unto himself. He was an absolute monarch while at sea. Some captains were kind and professional. Others were not. Some behaved with great dignity and grace while on shore, but at sea they seemed to undergo a transformation. Compared to some real-life monsters who commanded whaling ships out of New Bedford, Nantucket and other Yankee

Eight Hundred Brave Americans A-whaling for to Go

Killing a sperm whale with a lance about 1845.

ports, Melville's captain of the *Pequod,* Ahab, was sane and reasonable. One New Bedford skipper was brought up in court on his return from a three-year voyage on charges for using his men for target practice while they were stationed in the rigging. Another captain faced charges ashore for scrubbing a whaler down with a lye brick as a punishment during his most recent whaling voyage. When the prosecutor asked why he had done such a horrible thing, the captain responded that the man had engaged in mutiny. Of what did the mutiny consist, the prosecutor next asked. The indignant captain replied that the mutineer had presented himself on deck in his stocking feet! Whaling captains were a strange lot, far different from the average run of sea captains as a whole.

There were real mutinies on whaling ships to be sure. But they were not many, and one I can recall was actually quite funny. It happened on the whaling ship *Junior* out of New Bedford. The crew that the *Junior* had recruited was really quite seedy. They were truly lazy fellows who would not respond to anything but the most brutal treatment. They just hated all of the work in connection to the business of whaling. No group of malcontents was ever more determined to get out of what they considered to be a rotten situation. Whaling had proven to be far beyond their collective toleration, interest and ability, but they also did not have the fortitude to mutiny in the good old-fashioned way of slitting the captain's throat and tossing the mates overboard. They were just too terrified of the officers to do anything like that, but one fine night they came up with one certifiably crazy and most original idea.

In the dark of the night, they gathered up everything used to harpoon, capture, kill and try down a whale. Having gathered this vital material for the business of whaling, they tossed it all overboard. They even tossed the grinding wheel used to sharpen the cutting tools, harpoons, knives and lances into the deep. The next morning when whales were sighted in a pod, the call "there she blows" rang out from

The Yankee Fleet

Hoisting in the case and junk of a sperm whale about 1900.

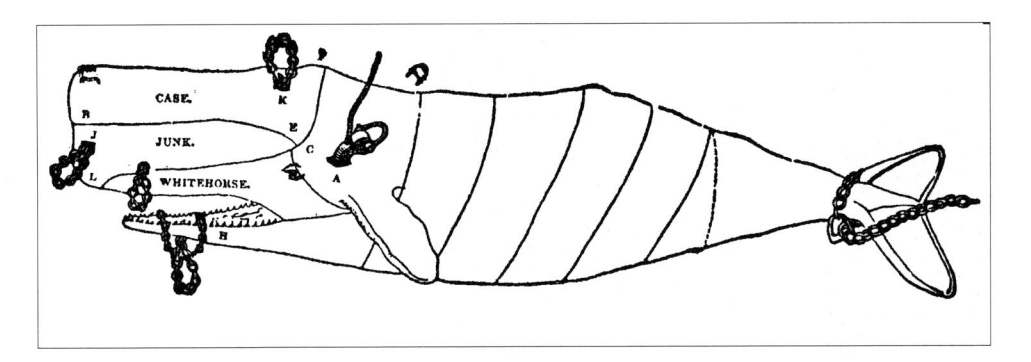

An old chart showing the plan for cutting up a sperm whale.

the masthead, but nothing could be done. Outside of the knives in the galley, there was nothing aboard the *Junior* that could do any harm to a whale. The captain, in a total fury, ordered the suspects put in irons until the nearest port could be reached. He set them ashore to get home the best way they could. The mutineers made their way to the nearest American consul and asked to be sent home as distressed seamen. So ended probably the most unusual mutiny in the history of whaling.

The business of whaling, for a business it was, has been greatly and overly romanticized. It has to be remembered that the whaling ship was a floating factory, slaughterhouse and rendering plant. It stunk to high heavens, and it was often said that a whaling ship could be smelled long before it could be seen. The captain and mates could be exceptionally brutal because they had the unenviable task of turning country boys and city bums attempting to escape the law into sailors. Many of these green hands had no idea of just what they were getting into, and they were often unwilling or lazy. The reason for the use of so many green hands or novice sailors on a whaling ship was that no real sailor would set out on more than one whaling voyage in a lifetime and that was most likely by accident. Therefore, the crews of whaling ships were not made up of prime sailors as a rule.

Just think of the facts of life aboard a ship engaged in this peculiar enterprise. Whaling voyages lasted from three to five years, and the crews were all but imprisoned on the ship during the whole of the voyage. The odyssey would not conclude until the ship was filled with oil. Only then would a whaler make for its home port. Another factor was that a whaling ship almost never entered a port in the first place. There was almost never any liberty given to the crew because desertion was epidemic in whaling. It was possible for a man to be confined on a ship 145 feet long with forty to sixty other human beings and never set foot on dry land for years at a time. As stated, reason for this was that most of the whalers would desert the ship if given the chance. This was also true of almost any sailing ship, but most prevalent among whalers. It is interesting to note that desertion from a merchant or whaling ship was a crime until the passage of the La Follette Seaman's Act in 1916.

The Yankee Fleet

Hoisting up the lower jaw of the well-toothed sperm whale.

Eight Hundred Brave Americans A-whaling for to Go

Sharks, or recruiting agents, would lure raw farm boys, runaways, petty criminals and the down and outers for a whaler's crew. These sharks would post signs in country towns and villages reading, "Eight Hundred young men wanted a-whaling for to go." Then the address of the shark's office would be printed on the posted handbill so that the young men would know where to report to sign up for a voyage. The raw or green hand would be enlisted and told when to report on board the whaling ship on such and such a day. At the time he reported aboard ship, he would sign articles in which he was promised compensation in the form of a "lay" or share of the ship's profits. This was the traditional method of compensation for a whaling voyage. The captain's share was almost always 10 percent. This provided a great incentive for him to do his best in filling the ship with oil. Most of the time, he was well worth it. The captain had to be as tough as nails, a good navigator, a good agent and businessman and very skilled in the business of killing, cutting in and trying down whale's blubber for oil. The average whaler would sign on for something like one seven-hundredth or so of the profit.

The kicker was that a common deckhand would have to buy everything he needed, including all of his clothing and even soap and knives, for the whole voyage from the ship's slop chest, which was like the company store where the prices were inflated to outrageous levels most of the time by captains who always knew how to squeeze an extra dime's profit out of the voyage. The poor green hand was overcharged for everything, and at the end of the whaling voyage whatever he was charged for the goods he bought during the voyage was deducted from his lay or share of the profits.

A story was told in a hundred-year-old book called *The Real Story of the Whaler* by A. Hyatt Verrill about one young man who shipped out of New Bedford, Massachusetts, and sailed for five years on a really horrible whaling voyage. This experience made Richard Henry Dana's *Two Years Before the Mast* look like a pleasure cruise. When the reluctant and much-abused and cheated whaler returned home, the oil and other whale products were sold. The time came for him to collect his lay. It amounted to exactly six dollars after the slop chest account was paid. The tight-lipped young man took his pitiful pay for five years of his life, went to a store and bought a pistol and some powder and shot. Then he loaded his gun and went off to settle some accounts of his own. He sought out the agent or shark who had placed the tantalizing advertisement in his local newspaper recruiting men for his voyage. On arriving at the agent's office, he entered and just shot the man dead without a word of explanation. I'm sure that the shark knew at the last seconds of his life just what it was all about.

The real professional deep-sea sailors on the whaling ship were the captain, the mates (three of them most of the time) and the harpooners (at least four of them). These were the only men onboard the ship who were there because they liked what they were doing. The harpooners might be African Americans, Native Americans or even Asians as well as white men. Race didn't seem to enter the picture unless a

The Yankee Fleet

A ship model of an old-time whaler showing sperm whale carcass set up for the cutting in.

ship should happen to enter a southern port. In Charleston, for example, free black sailors had to spend the time that their ship was in port locked up in the city jail! Good old racism was ever busy south of the Mason-Dixon line in the age of slavery. Only real ability counted when it came to the exacting skills needed to take whales. These vital positions were highly paid and attracted individuals willing to make several voyages especially if the captain was a friend or was well known for being fair, or even better, had a reputation for being very lucky. That was not the case of one rather morose captain by the name of Moses Snell who was the master of the ship *Archer* out of New Bedford. Here begins his story taken from the pages of his very own log.

The voyage of the *Archer* began on May 27, 1845, from the port of New Bedford, Massachusetts. As one reads Captain Snell's log, everything seems to be going well until the entry of September 8 of that year. On that date the Captain writes,

> *This is to certify that I Moses Snell master of the ship Archer have this day at 8 AM been informed by almost my whole crew, that Thomas Miller carpenter, is fully*

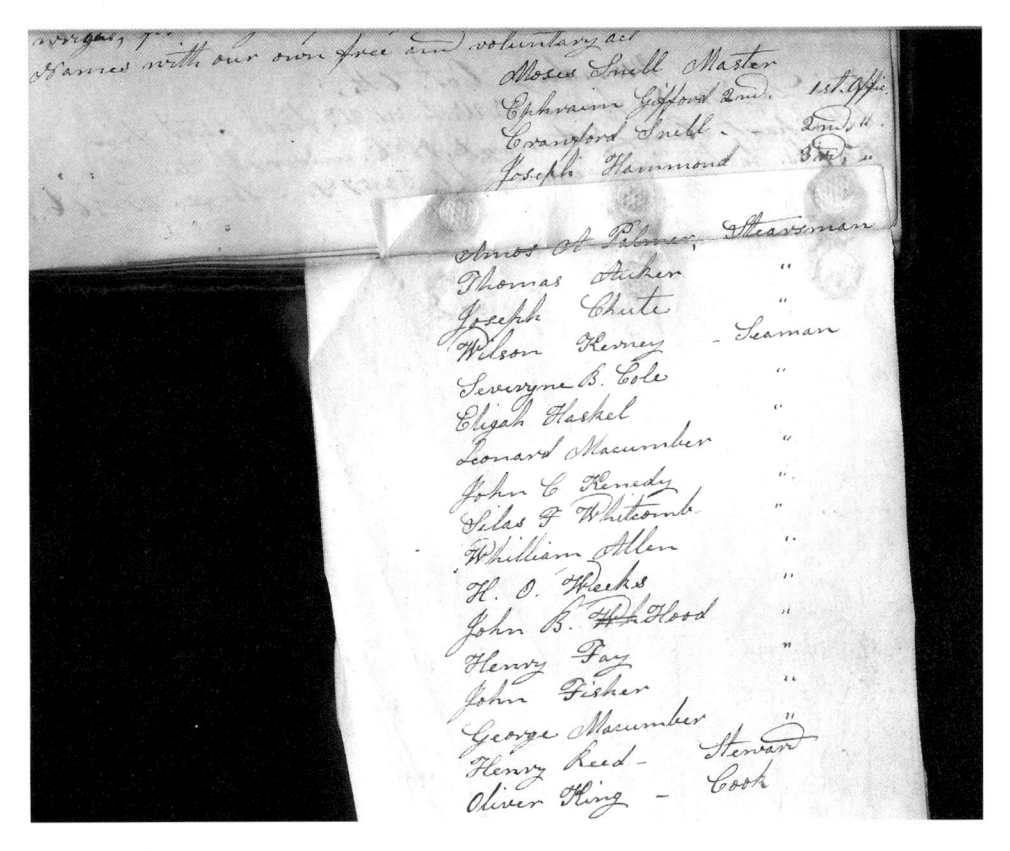

Eight Hundred Brave Americans A-whaling for to Go

Page from the *Archer* showing the names forged by Captain Snell.

> *disposed to break my orders, and destroy all good order and discipline on board said ship, by profane swearing, fighting, and repeatedly making threats, and not only that but often said that he only wanted a certain number to join him in his evil designs, and he would deny duty and abused the crew for not joining him, he also proposed hauling down the fore castle steps and said he would kill the first officer who came down the gangway, I have also found him to be an abusive man to me and my mate from time to time, without any provocation whatever, under all these considerations I have deemed it highly necessary to punish him for his mutinous conduct, accordingly I have inflicted reasonable punishment on the body of said Miller and for the safety of myself and the crew, and the good of the voyage have put him in confinement.*

I think that a sad picture is beginning to emerge of the captain's mindset at this point of his narrative. He appears as a highly disturbed man. For example, Snell allowed no swearing, card playing, singing, drinking or dancing, or as I can see, any recreation for his twenty-man crew. About the dancing: Sailors liked to dance the hornpipe with their arms folded or crossed on their chests to music provided by crewmen who could play an accordion, pipes, harmonica or a fiddle. Even Captain Bligh knew the value of entertainment of this sort and hired a man to play the fiddle on the voyage of the HMS *Bounty* for the amusement of his crew and for purposes of keeping up morale. Too bad it didn't work for him.

Snell must have been acting under the effect of some extreme hang-ups based on his strict religious scruples in formulating some of his more unreasonable rules. But for men to be cooped up in the little sea-going world of the *Archer* for almost three years, this lack of recreation had to incite a fine madness in all aboard the vessel. One thing I do know is that sailors on this voyage did engage in the time honored craft of scrimshawing. This folk art consists of carving whale tooth or bone into gifts for loved ones back home. I have, in addition to the log of the *Archer*, two scrimshaws actually made on this voyage. One is a memorial to a sailor who died, and the other shows a whaling ship, the *Archer*. They also smoked a lot of tobacco in several forms.

The "reasonable punishment" referred to in the log must have been a flogging, and confinement of Miller must have been to an extremely small space not too much bigger than a closet. The language of the log is also oddly legalistic in its tone. I think that Snell, apart from being just a tad mad, was also intent on covering himself in case of any future questioning or investigation of his conduct in the Miller matter by the forces of the law. He may even have feared a future court case. His log shows that he was somewhat delusional and paranoid. Today I think that he might be diagnosed as being bipolar.

To understand his thought process, one must read what follows the September 8 entry regarding the punishment of Miller. "We the undersigned do solomley declare that the above is a true description of the character of the said Miller and are witness to the above mentioned, and consider the punishment to be just and wright, for the good of all parties whereunto we have given our names with our own free and voluntary act."

The English is a bit irregular, but the message is very clear. Captain Snell badly felt the need to be justified in what he had done. To seek validation, he faked the signatures of the crew under this entry of September 29, 1845, which relates the Miller story. The signatures of the twenty crew members match his own handwriting. The handwriting is also identical to that of the log. Why had the crew not signed the log themselves? Maybe the answer was to be found in the entries written over the next two years. From the log, we discover that Ephraim Gifford was his first mate, his brother Crawford Snell was second mate and Joseph Hammond was third mate. None of them seem willing either to defy him or back him up. Even his brother Crawford turns on him altogether. Later on we learn that there are two mutinies against the strangely despotic rule of Captain Moses Snell. One is led by his own brother and second officer Crawford Snell. The story becomes even more confusing because the family removed a vital page to prevent the whole truth from becoming fully known. When I bought the log and scrimshaws back in 1978, I asked

Eight Hundred Brave Americans A-whaling for to Go

SYMBOLS USED BY WHALEMEN IN THEIR LOG-BOOKS.

1—Sperm whale. 2—Right whale or bowhead. 3—Grampus.
4—Porpoise. 5—Boat lowered. 6—Flukes up "sounded."
7—Drew (escaped).

Symbols used by whalemen in their logbooks.

The Yankee Fleet

The engraving *Last of the Whale Ships* appeared in Drakes's *Nooks and Corners of the New England Coast* in 1875. Whaling still had a half century to run, but it really was a doomed industry by 1875.

the captain's great-great-nephew if he knew what the missing pages contained. He could only reply that they had been destroyed because of the sensibilities of some of his older relatives, and he further stated that we were lucky that the whole thing had not been burned.

The captain stood alone against the crew for whom he must have made the ship a living hell. This can be assumed when Snell records in the log that his boat was stove in by a whale and that he had to rescue himself because nobody would help him. He also records that he had lockjaw and almost died, but once again there was no help offered to him. Additionally Snell received a letter in Hawaii informing him that his wife had died, which sends him into a deep depression, and he rambles on for pages, pouring out his heartfelt grief and wallowing in profound sorrow.

The horrible voyage ended on Saturday, October 9, 1847. He had been out at sea for two years, four months and ten days. He also returned with very little oil to show for all of his miserable time whaling. The investors, who had laid out some substantial sums of money on this venture, must not have been too pleased with this unhappy captain. On examining the log's conclusion, one thing jumps out at me. The captain was an honest man when it came to material issues. Total sales out of the slop chest were only $132.49. The crew bought 275 pounds of oil soap at 3¾ cents a pound for a total of $10.31. It must have taken a lot of soap to get the smell of the whales out of your nostrils. A box of soap bars was also sold to the ship's crew at 6½ cents a bar for a total of $4.87. This was pretty expensive. Eight sheath knives were sold for 10½ cents each for a total of 84 cents; 660 pounds of tobacco were sold from the slop chest during the voyage for a total of $66.

Smoking was the one vice left to the men, and they did a lot of it at 10 cents a pound; 2,350 "cegars" were sold for a grand total of $4.70. Additionally, 227 pounds of some other soap were sold at 6½ cents a pound for a total of $14.75. The *Archer* must have been an uncommonly clean ship crewed by sailors wearing the cleanest clothes in the Pacific. Six pairs of shoes were sold at 90 cents a pair for a total of $5.40. Most of the crew must have been barefoot. A single pair of pumps (dancing shoes or low cut shoes more often worn on formal occasions) sold for 60 cents. Two pairs of stockings were sold at two shillings a pair for a total of 67 cents.

At this point, it might be a good idea to discuss coinage. Until 1857, European and South American gold and silver coinage circulated in the United States side by side with the national coinage. One could still find items priced in shillings, pounds, pence, florins, crowns and guineas. By 1857, the Revolution had been over for seventy-four years, and Congress correctly thought that it was high time to use our own coinage exclusively. Therefore, foreign gold and silver coinage was demonetized in 1857. To continue with the slop chest sales, forty-eight striped cotton shirts were sold at 48 cents each for a total of $23.04. Six tin pans were sold for 20 cents each for a total of $1.20, and lastly two spoons were sold to crew members for 3 cents each. Total sales, as noted, were $132.49. These sales provide a small peek into the sailor's world.

A substantial stock of goods remained unsold, including spoons, tin pots, tin pans, comforters, stockings, mitts, Scotch caps, Guernsey frocks, vests, a round jacket, drawers, blankets, duck pants, duck frocks, calico shirts, shoes, pumps, belts and sheaths, Rogers knives, sheath knives, thread, hard soap, pipes and oil soap, valued at $279.83. This unsold material also gives a look into life aboard ship.

Many voyages didn't go so badly. A lot of whalers enjoyed successful voyages of only three years duration and returned to port with from fifteen hundred to three thousand or more barrels of oil, tons of whalebone and some ambergris. A lot depended on the capacity of the ship when it came to the amount of oil brought back to market, as well as luck. Sperm oil was the best and came from the whale that put up the hardest fight. The mighty sperm whale was from sixty to eighty-something feet long. In most cases, its size depended on its age and nutrition. The sperm whale was one of two major types of whales taken, which actually had teeth. Those teeth are located in the lower jaw only. The other toothed-whale is the killer

The Yankee Fleet

Scrimshaw of the mid-eighteenth century.

whale, which is only a little fellow of fifteen to twenty-five feet in length as an adult. They tend not to be dangerous to humans for the most part.

The jaws of the sperm whale were sixteen to twenty-two feet long on average in the adult. The whale was capable of biting a twenty-two-foot-long whaleboat in half or reducing it to bits by chewing it. This gave rise to the slogan, "A stove boat or a dead whale." The actual harpooning of the whale has been touched upon, but some of the fine points of actually harpooning the beast are best imagined if you place yourself in the whaleboat with the men doing the job. First of all, confronting the sperm whale in all of its mighty reality would be frightening even if you started off in a small way with a right whale of forty-five to fifty-something feet in length. The earliest whalers called the right whale by this name because it was the "right whale" to catch. Right whales are relatively docile animals, which tend not to put up a big fight when harpooned, but their oil was inferior to that of a sperm whale and commanded an inferior price.

The right whale does not have teeth. It strains its food, mostly made up of krill and other small sea life, through baleen that hangs down at the front of the mouth. Baleen was used in strips as corset stays. Small boxes were also made of baleen somewhat in the style of Shaker boxes. They were made as gifts for the home folks or sweethearts of the sailors who hoped that they were still available on their return. Corsets were a fixture in the women's wear trade in an age when the well-dressed woman cultivated the famed hourglass shape in pursuit of high fashion.

The whales did not yield up their useful body parts easily. The sperm whale was a fighter. When a sperm whale was struck, there was always going to be a Nantucket sleigh ride in store. The whales would dive, stove in boats and go after sailors in the water, tossing them about like dolls, and sometimes, after wreaking havoc, escape altogether. The whaler had to tire the great behemoths out, wear them down, and at last, lance them. This meant rowing up to the whale and stabbing it in the heart, in the brain through the eye or in the lungs with a razor-sharp lance. In fact, harpooners liked to brag that they could shave with their lance heads. Killing the whale was not an easy job, and it almost always fell to the mate to do this. In fact, it was a point of honor to give the whale the coup de grace.

The whale would then have to be towed back to the ship for the cutting in, the process by which the blubber would be taken from the body of the whale for trying down into oil in the tryworks. Sometimes during the hunt, the whale would tow the boat so far from the ship that the whale and the whaleboat might actually be picked up by another whaling ship twenty miles away from the original vessel. Other times the whale might tow the boat so far from the whaler that the men were never to be seen again. In the normal course of business, the whale would sometimes arrive at its destination with a following of hungry sharks who would feast on the carcass while the men went to work on cutting it up for processing. One slip and a whaler could end up as a shark's snack as the ferocious carnivores tore into the whale.

The sperm whale would be decapitated with razor-sharp spades as it lay in the water close by the ship, and then it would be hauled into position to be hung upside down, suspended by chains from the spars. The best oil was to be found in the head in the case or brains of the sperm whale. This part of the whale is called the junk. This oil would be used to make the best candles and lubricants for clockworks, music boxes and fine machinery. Old whalers would laugh and say, "His brain is all oil." In fact, the contents of the case could just be bailed out in buckets. This was not a sweet job, although some of the men liked to dip bread into this oil and eat it. Most likely they were out at sea so long that they thought this was a delicacy. The blubber would be cut from the whale's carcass in long, wide and thick strips weighing hundreds of pounds with flensing knives that looked like wide chisels mounted on long poles. Blubber hooks attached to ropes or chains and passing through blocks would be

The Whalemen's Bethel and Seamen's Home in New Bedford about 1895.

attached to the separated huge strips of blubber and then hoisted to the deck, which was running red with mammalian blood that in turn drained into the scuppers.

These strips would then be cut into chunks called horse pieces. Another knife would then be used to slice into the horse pieces about one-third to three-fourths through in parallel slices. Because the results suggested the pages of a book, the sliced horse pieces were now called bible leaves. On the deck, there was a brick structure, often but not always built on an iron foundation, called a tryworks. A fire was built under the great boiling pots built into the tryworks, and the bible leaves, with their nice parallel slits, were tossed into the pot to have the oil boiled out of them. The slitting of the horse pieces allowed the oil to boil out of the blubber easier. The refined oil was then transferred into the barrels below decks. A sperm whale might yield from sixty to a hundred barrels depending on its size and physical condition. Old whales, thin and on the verge of death, were not worth the effort of killing for the tiny amount of oil they might render. As they entered extreme old age, they often used up their reserves of fat.

Ambergris was a highly valued, greasy, yellowish substance found in the digestive system of a whale that had swallowed something distressing like the beak of a cuttlefish, a giant squid or some other obstruction that caused discomfort. This in turn, causes the ambergris to form. There was an old saying that a handful of ambergris could buy a farm. This material was used as a fixative for scent in the best perfumes and was therefore of huge economic value. In *Moby Dick*, one of the mates seeks out an old sick whale just because he might have ambergris in him. The mate proves to be right. After the whale or whales were tried down for their oil, the ship would be scrubbed down until the next catch. After this workout, it becomes apparent just how popular the soap in the slop chest would be.

There were a lot of whalemen who never returned from sea, and sometimes there would be whole ships that never returned to port. They were swallowed up by the rapacious ocean, which gave so much and often demanded a hefty tribute in return. In New Bedford at the Seaman's Bethel, known as the Whalemen's Chapel in *Moby Dick*, there are many memorials that commemorate men lost at sea. These go back well into the 1700s. Nobody knows just how many of these men and their ships were lost after being rammed by an outraged whale. There are enough survivors of such incidents to know that these things happened. A wounded whale more than half as long as a ship, a beast of sixty to eighty feet in length weighing as much as some oceangoing vessels of the time, was an opponent not to be taken lightly. A wounded whale was a huge, intelligent, battering ram with a will of iron to match the will of its hunters and was often motivated by having a score to settle with the men who attempted to injure it at each human encounter. Once one of these behemoths decided that the ship itself was the source of its painful troubles, the obvious solution became the killing of the ship or driving it off by ramming it.

Recent studies have shown just how intelligent these giants are. They communicate over the vast ocean. They sing their songs, with the meanings known only to them. They even sell hundreds of thousands of CD recordings, which indicates their charm. Perhaps they could use a really good agent. Doing away with a source of danger to them, once identified as a whaling ship, is not beyond their intellectual ability. Such was the case with the whaling ship *Essex*.

On August 12, 1819, the whaling ship *Essex* departed from the port of Nantucket. By 1819, it was recognized that the best whaling was in the Pacific because the Atlantic held mostly the less profitable right whales, and their populations had been on the decline for years. The real money lay in the western waters of the world's largest ocean. Passage to Cape Horn was relatively smooth. Rounding the cape presented no great problems such as those experienced by the *Bounty* thirty-two years before when Captain William Bligh had spent some thirty days in a vain effort to beat his way around the cape through the Strait of Magellan. In the end he had to give it up, turn about and sail west around the southern tip of Africa, the Cape of Good Hope, in order to reach Tahiti to get the breadfruit plants that were his mission.

The *Essex* enjoyed clear sailing to the whaling grounds where Captain Pollard had always enjoyed some success. All was going well, and on November 29, the call of, "There she blows," rang out loud and clear from the lookout on high. A large sperm whale had been sighted that would easily yield more than a hundred barrels of fine oil. The captain's boat was lowered along with those of his three officers. All four whaleboats made for the monster. The first to arrive was that of the first mate. The harpooner struck the beast hard, but no sooner had the whale felt the iron than it lashed out with its flukes and stove in the first mate's boat. This sort of thing was not unknown in the world of whaling. The men were instructed to remove their jackets and stuff them into the holes in the boat's damaged planking. The mate then ordered the men to bail out the water as the boat limped back to the *Essex*.

While this adventure was being played out, the captain and second mate had already both struck the whale and were giving battle to it. The first mate in the meantime swung the ship in their direction and headed toward the fight while his men concentrated their efforts on the repair of their boat. In the interval, the whale broke away from the captain and second mate and dove under the waves. It was obvious to the captain and the mate that this was no ordinary whale. Its behavior was unlike any they had ever seen before. It was big, old and wise in the ways of the humans who were after it. The whale had met their kind before. Those encounters were imprinted on its memory along with who knows how many escapes. It had never been unable to get away. The captain looked at his second mate. He was sure that the whale was at least eighty-five feet long. It was the largest whale he had ever seen or most likely was ever to see. It had been there in front of him, and now it was gone in a flash.

But that was only for the moment. It once again breached and swam on the surface of the glassy sea. What happened next was all too unreal. The great whale rested for a moment as if it was sizing up its options. Then, as if seized by all the pent up rage of its scores of years, the monster surged in the direction of the oncoming *Essex*. The great whale struck just at the catheads, staving in the ship's heavy planking and thus letting in the sea. The whale seemed a bit stunned at first. Then it seemed to have recovered as it dove and then reappeared. It seemed to gather up its strength once again for one last assault on the ship. The whale sped ahead in a wild dash and struck the ship again with all its might. The unbelieving men watched in horror as their haven of safety, thousands of miles from nowhere, was suddenly all but taken from them. The great whale swam under the ship then resurfaced as if mocking them. Then the ancient leviathan swam away to another world where it was the absolute king of all the ocean it spanned in its wanderings. The whale left

Eight Hundred Brave Americans A-whaling for to Go

A 1910 whaling schooner.

The Yankee Fleet

The sinking of the bark *Kathleen* after being rammed by a whale in 1901.

mere mortals in its mighty wake who were small and insignificant after all. They were left to contemplate the ruins of their little manufactured world.

Pollard kept his head, ordered the boats back to the stricken ship and then ordered the masts cut away. The impact of the whale had left the *Essex* on its beam ends tilting horribly. Now that the masts were cut away, the ship righted itself. The men pumped with all their might, but it was very clear that the ship was finished. Pollard ordered the decks scuttled and stores taken from below to supply the boats with what food and water could be rescued. They had to ready themselves for a very long voyage. Pollard had four boats, one of which had been stove in. For three days, while the ship engaged in a losing fight to live, Pollard worked his men hard to repair the damaged boat, to no avail, and to make all the remaining small craft seaworthy. By the end of the third day, the holes in *Essex* were greatly enlarged. The ship was on the verge of breaking up, and the weather was beginning to change harshly. In the end only three of the four boats were seaworthy enough to set out on the three-thousand-mile voyage to Peru, which was the closest landfall of which Pollard was aware.

Pollard and his men set out on November 23, 1819, on what might be the last adventure of their lives. Day after day, exposed to the weather, the men worked at the oars in an effort to row to safety. I doubt if any of them thought that they would make it, but they had to try. The little food and water that was rescued and taken from the ship was stretched beyond reason. The men grew weaker and weaker. Yet on they plied the oars ever eastward to South America. After five days, an island was sighted. There was little security to be found there by the look of it. In the Pacific there was always a chance that the inhabitants of any of the islands might just see the white men as exotic fare or an interesting snack before a large banquet. As the men neared the island, Pollard claimed it to be Ducie Island, which he knew to be uninhabited.

There were only some seabirds and a few shellfish to eat and no fresh water to be found there. After a period of rest on the dry land, Pollard and his men set out again in their open boats. The date was December 27. Some few of the men elected to stay on the island. They preferred to die in the comparative comfort of a wave-washed shore than in a boat covered with blisters. They didn't like the prospect of burning up in the daytime and freezing at night on the open sea. The tortures of hunger and thirst in an open boat held no charms for them. Pollard had understood this and wished them well.

The remaining men of the *Essex*'s company had a horrible row of 2,500 miles to their next landfall, which was Juan Fernandez. On January 29, 1820, the second mate died, and two days later the boats all became separated in a storm. As the men in the boats that had been separated from Pollard died, their arms and legs were removed from their bodies and used for food. In Captain Pollard's boat the sailor Chase became ill. As the day passed under the drying sun, Chase went out of his mind. He called for his dinner and his cup as if ashore in a New England waterside tavern. He raved on and on about food and drink until the crew could stand it no longer. They threw a piece of canvass over him, and that seemed to quiet him down. At sunset, he died. Nobody in Pollard's boat had tasted human flesh up to that point, but they were all nearly at the end of their strength, and hunger obsessed their every thought. The thought had crossed all their minds, but nobody actually spoke of eating Chase's flesh until the sailor Brazali Ray articulated that awful reality which everybody had privately entertained. The others simply agreed and resigned to the horrible inevitability. Chase's limbs were cut from his body, and the torso was consigned to the deep.

Several days passed and there were now only four men left in Pollard's boat. The body of Chase had been used up, and they had not come so far only to give up and die now. It was decided to draw lots to see who would die to feed the rest. The lots were drawn, and the lot that meant death fell to the teenage cabin boy, Owen Coffin, Pollard's nephew and favorite. The Captain was aghast. He drew his pistol and yelled, "I'll kill the first man who puts his hands on that boy!"

Coffin then said, "No, I like my lot well enough. It's my right to die. I drew the short stick."

Pollard tried to convince his nephew that he would take his place, but young Coffin insisted. The boy placed his head on the side of the boat so that the shot that killed him would not harm the craft. Ray volunteered to do the killing. Pollard turned away, and Ray fired the fatal shot. Coffin was then cut up and consumed by these good Christian men driven half mad with hunger and thirst. On February 17, 1820, the first mate's boat was sighted by the English vessel *Indian*, which was

The Yankee Fleet

The whaling schooner *Amelia* of New Bedford.

a merchant brig. Five days later, a ship, the *Dauphin* of Nantucket, sighted Pollard's sorry boat and rescued the two remaining men. It seems that Ray in his turn had died and was eaten by Pollard and Charles Ramsdale. They didn't mention too many details of their survival aboard the rescue ship. Under the circumstances that was quite understandable.

Pollard went to sea after awhile and was subsequently shipwrecked. He was rescued after only a few days in an open boat and vowed never to go to sea again. He returned to Nantucket and swallowed the anchor (gave up the sea) and secured a job as a night watchman for the town. The story of the *Essex* was told in whispers. Nobody wanted to seem like they were interested in the facts of the case, but of course they all were. The tale of the rammed ship and the eating of human flesh and the ethics of it were discussed in the all but silent houses of Nantucket in hushed tones. When Pollard died, barrels of ship's hardtack and crackers were found in the attic of his house. He lived in mortal fear that he would be forced by hunger to taste human flesh again. Charles Ramsdale did go back to the sea and eventually became a ship's master. It is said that the story of the *Essex* inspired Herman Melville's classic tale of a ship sunk by a whale, which is the definitive novel about whaling.

The *Charles W. Morgan* ashore circa 1900. This grand old whaling ship has been well restored and can be seen in a museum setting at Mystic Seaport in Connecticut.

The Yankee Fleet

The Last of the New Bedford Whaling Fleet. Circa 1915.

The whaler *Kathleen* was sailing about the West Indies not far from the Leeward Islands in 1901 when a whale was sighted. The boats were lowered and set off in a chase for the whale. After a bit, the whale was struck, but it pulled away. In a moment, the whale turned on the ship and struck it with all of its might. The ship's timbers were stove in, and the ship filled with water. The remarkable thing about this from a historian's perspective is that somebody actually took a photograph of the ship in the act of sinking. Land was not far off, and nobody had to be eaten.

In 1859, a Captain Drake found oil in the town of Titusville, Pennsylvania. This discovery helped to put an end to whaling. During the Civil War, the United States government tried to close the port of Charleston by sinking the great Stone Fleet, composed largely of whaling ships, at the harbor's mouth. In 1871 and 1872, most of the Arctic whaling fleet was crushed by ice in one of the coldest winters ever recorded in history. By the dawn of the twentieth century, most of the whaling industry was carried on in small vessels like the *John Manta*, which was rigged like a sloop. Only the *Charles W. Morgan* is left of the hundreds of nineteenth-century United States whalers that once dominated that industry worldwide.

Thousands of other relics remain like scrimshawed whale teeth, sailor's valentines made of shells worked into wonderful designs in hinged shadowbox frames, swifts used to wind yarn and pie crimpers or cutters with fantastic handles carved in the shape of greyhounds, sea horses and other fanciful figures. Other items were also made for the home folks like games of dominoes, whalebone clothespins and scrimshawed busks decorated by sailors and used to keep lady's corsets stiff in front and to hold her body in good and fashionable shape. All of these artifacts were kept by thousands of people to whom they were given as gifts when whalers returned home. These treasured pieces of true American folk art were made on those impossibly long voyages dedicated to the chase of the whale. No doubt all scrimshawing activity kept more than a few sailors from going totally bonkers on those confining little ships for three years or more. In the end, this wonderful folk art produced by the sailors is the most outstanding contribution of this trade in whale. The oil is long gone, but the art of the whaler remains.

Chapter 8

The American Century of Sail

By 1815, the United States had been building the best sailing ships in the world. The British first sea lord, who commanded the mightiest fleets in the world, had ordered British frigates not to engage their American counterparts in a one-on-one basis during the War of 1812. England and the United States were never to try their strength against each other again in war, but commerce was another matter altogether. England became the greatest producer of iron in the 1700s. Germany overtook England in the 1870s, and the United States outstripped the Germans in iron and steel production by 1900. But the golden age of wooden ships, for a time, was the property of the United States. The winning of the iconic yachting prize, the America's Cup, by the United States in 1851 symbolized the country's superiority in wooden ship construction and the perfection of sail.

The USS *Constitution* epitomized wooden warship construction by the time it first went on station in 1798. It had been preceded by the Baltimore clippers as an example of great American commercial innovation. A long series of different vessels would demonstrate American genius and innovation in the sophisticated development of wooden sailing vessels. In Massachusetts, the thirty-ton schooner *Fame* was constructed as a commercial fishing vessel, but its speed and intrinsic strength made ship an ideal raider and privateer during the War of 1812. In its early career, *Fame* captured the three-hundred-ton British vessel *Concord*, which was on its way to England. Later the *Elbe* was also taken by *Fame*. Such prizes made its owner, Captain Upton, more wealthy. *Fame* has been reproduced in exact detail and can be seen in Salem, Massachusetts, today.

As innovative as the ships I have mentioned were, no ship made up to this time was more beautiful than *Cleopatra's Barge*. Salem's merchant prince, George Crowninshield set out to build the most wonderful yacht ever envisioned. Of course he had to call this lushly appointed craft *Cleopatra's Barge*. No other name could so perfectly reflect its sheer luxury. Only the best craftsmen were employed in its construction and the furnishing of its appointments. The mahogany woodwork, the

The Yankee Fleet

The island of Nantucket in 1870 as seen from sea.

high-style federal furniture, the rich silks and lush velvets and all the other bits and pieces of its fantastic furnishings made the ultra sleek vessel a wonder to behold. Crowninshield had hoped to attract royalty as guests upon his yacht. He was the ultimate social climber, but he discovered that mere toys, no matter how grand, could not buy him introductions into the highest social strata, an introduction to which he so desired. But all was not lost. At least he had built a floating dream that fired the imagination, and he got to sail to Europe to show off his magnificent folly. This was a good thing because he died within a year of his grand voyage on the world's most beautiful ship, and at least he got to enjoy his boat.

Yankees always liked their pleasure craft. It did not have to be a fancy affair like *Cleopatra's Barge* with mahogany furniture or silk cushions. It could be a rowboat that just allowed an escape from the mainland. In Puritan times, men liked to row or sail out to Nantucket to kick up their heels and get away from the ministers and their spies, the tithing men, who informed for the parson. Once these refugees from Sunday services were off pretending to be fishing, they could cross over to Nantucket and have a good time among the more tolerant Quakers.

In a theocracy like Massachusetts Bay Colony, one had to act the model Puritan twenty four hours a day. The tithing men were constantly spying in order to report every transgression they saw back to the minister so that he could reveal everybody's wrongdoings during Sunday services. Now if you played your cards right, you could sail off fishing in the general direction of Nantucket on Saturday and arrange it so that you would not return until Monday and be spared the Sabbath altogether. One could always say that one got blown out to sea, went out too far or got stranded on the island and could not get back until the tide turned. All of these excuses were sound, and unless some snoop was around or somebody slipped up, everything would be fine.

Nantucket was always a fun place to get away to. It was a different world from Massachusetts. In 1860, *Harper's Magazine* published a story about an amazing

The American Century of Sail

View of the town and shoreline of Nantucket from a widow's walk about 1870.

Whale houses of Siasconset as seen by a *Harper's Magazine* artist in 1860.

character who lived on the island by the name of Mother Cary. The following is taken directly from pages 747 and 748 of the 1860 edition of *Harper's New Monthly Magazine* from a true story called "A Summer in New England."

Our shouts opened the door of a tenement near at hand, from which an old cripple issued, and shuffling towards us with great eagerness, offered to take our horse. We yielded the reins readily, and inquired if there was a house of entertainment in the place.

"Certainly," said he, "jist you go in there [indicating the low door from which he had sallied], *and Mistress Cary will entertain you as nice as need be."*

We entered and found ourselves in a cuddy, measuring about eight by ten, which, in addition to its capacity as a public reception room of the hotel, also seem to serve as a general store house of groceries, provisions, and fancy goods of varied character. By a cursory glance I was enabled to inventory a portion of the contents, as follows: Dried codfish, bottled beer, sugar candy, fishing lines, and hooks, eggs, whiskey, ginger cakes, opodeldoc, pork, cigars, cheese, Radway's Ready Relief, tobacco, ship biscuit, Pain Killer, jack-knives, Lucifer matches, and jewelry.

The prospect was not so bad. The house was well provisioned at least; as tidy as could be expected under the circumstances, and besides, the most delicate olfactories could not have detected the slightest smell of any kind, except dried codfish: but if folks are squeamish on this or other subjects, they had better stay home, and be content to do their traveling through Harper's Magazine. As no one appeared to receive us, Dick thumped upon the glass case that contained the fancy goods, jewelry, and ginger cakes, and forthwith from a side door entered a little old woman with a motherly vinegar aspect who saluted us sharply with,

"Well, what have ye got to sell?"

"Nothing at all," replied Dick, depositing upon a chair the knapsack which contained our baggage.

"Then," quoth she, "Take your traps and tramp."

"Madam," said I with mildness, yet assuming some slight dignity of manner," We are strangers who have come a-pleasuring to this famous place, and have been informed that you could entertain us for the day perhaps."

"Oh, that's it is it? That's quite another thing. Set down sirs and rest yourselves, and we'll see what we can do for you."

The old woman looked mollified, but to remove the disadvantageous impression that we were pedestrians, I continued.

"Our horse and carriage has been attended to by your husband."

"My husband!" exclaimed Mother Cary. "My husband?"

"Madam, I allude to the lame gentleman who took our horse and promised to have him fed."

Our hostess stood for a moment speechless, as if undecided weather she should put me to death a la basilisk, or annihilate me with a package of codfish which lay

Mother Elizabeth Cary from *Harper's Magazine* in 1860. Take note of the not so fashionable turban decorating Mistress Cary's head.

> *near at hand. At length she shrieked out, like an angered sea gull, "My husband, did you say? Gentlemen did you call him?—That creature that I hired from the alms house to attend to people's horses! I guess your eyesight is not very good sir, or you must be strangers in this country. I am Mistress Elizabeth Cary, at your service. My husband! Faugh! I thank God that I'm not that low yet!"*
>
> *And in high disdain she flounced out of the room.*

Needless to say things got patched up after Mother Cary returned in her silks and satins to serve dinner and arrange for a boat so that the writer for *Harper's* and his

The Yankee Fleet

The *Sandy Hook* lightship circa 1870.

cousin could enjoy their vacation on Nantucket in that summer of 1860, which was the last summer before the Civil War was to break out. The *Harper's* depiction of Mother Cary is interesting as she sits in her antique turban that passed out of fashion a score years before. She is a Nantucket type whose image has been reproduced many times before, but here she is, the undiluted original almost 150 years after her image was first published. The writer's voyage was far from the glamour of the one taken by George Crowninshield on *Cleopatra's Barge*, but I bet that the writer and his cousin enjoyed their trip more.

Rhode Island born Captain Robert Gray opened a fantastic chapter in Yankee navigational history with his voyages to the great American northwest to trade for furs and other products. By sea, the West Coast could only be reached by going around the Horn through the Strait of Magellan and then north, up past the coasts of South, Central and North America. Gray had entered into a partnership with another Yankee by the name of Captain John Kendrick. In 1789, they spent time in the Oregon Country gathering up a substantial number of valuable pelts. These furs were then transported to the Chinese port of Canton. This was the beginning of the very rich Old China Trade.

China was seen as the most exotic country in the world. Marco Polo's book of his travels to China in the thirteenth century excited the imagination of Europe.

The American Century of Sail

Trial of the bomb and life line during a drill at a lifeboat station circa 1880.

This in turn fueled the Age of Discovery, which was to result in the discovery and colonization of the Americas. China reached its greatest prestige during the reign of Emperor Ch'ien-lung who reigned from 1736 to 1796. Wallpaper, printed cloth and European porcelain celebrated western admiration for all things Chinese. The Old China Trade led to a collecting mania in Europe of Chinese porcelain in the 1500s through the early 1800s. The French, Germans, Dutch and English all tried to copy it. The men of New England went right to China for the porcelain, bringing furs, sandalwood and opiates to trade for it, as well as for tea, ginger and other spices.

Gray opened the American trade with China, and others would follow in sturdy and ever improving Yankee built ships. One fact has always amazed me, and that is how trading voyages were financed. Anyone who wanted to could invest in a trading venture. Rich merchants could consign goods to be traded; widows could invest their savings of ten dollars; and sailors could invest along with Yankee farmers and shopkeepers. The whole community was always materially interested in the outcome of these early trading voyages. Granite paving stones quarried in Quincy, Massachusetts, would serve as the ballast of a ship. When the cargo of that ship was sold in Canton or some other Chinese port, that ballast would also be sold. Today many a Chinese road is paved with stone brought from Massachusetts by these early trading vessels.

When the merchant ships returned to Boston, Salem and the other Yankee ports, an auction of the goods bought in China would be advertised in the journals. On the appointed day, the new ballast, consisting of Chinese porcelain in barrels, would be auctioned off. The paving stones had been replaced as ballast, namely by all those heavy barrels of Chinese porcelain. Six-color Canton (or rose medallion china), blue and white Canton ware, Fitzhugh china, rose Canton ware and other decorated porcelain—today valued from a hundred to many thousands of dollars a piece—would be auctioned off at an average of four cents per individual item, but whatever it brought, it was a good deal better than the cost of stone ballast. There was no part of those little Yankee ships that didn't pay.

The Yankee Fleet

The customhouse and port at Salem, Massachusetts, circa 1835. Nathaniel Hawthorne labored here as a civil servant.

When the sales were concluded, every investor was paid his share of the profit after the commissions and costs were deducted. The widow who invested her ten dollars might very well receive thirty or more back if the voyage was a success. The faster a ship could sail, the greater the return, because more voyages could be made. A voyage to China and back was a trip of one- to two-years' duration. Given the life expectancy of the time, investors were concerned about living to see the profits from their venture.

Donald McKay would greatly improve the prospects of American trade in wooden sailing vessels. He was born in Nova Scotia in 1810 and learned the shipbuilding trade well. By 1841, he was in Massachusetts in Newburyport where he established a shipyard. In 1845, McKay moved to an even larger operation in East Boston where he built revolutionary vessels of extreme grace, speed and sleekness, which became known as clippers because of how they clipped along at fifteen to twenty knots under full sail in a good wind. During the Gold Rush of 1849, his ship, *Flying Cloud*, broke all records to San Francisco by sailing there from New York in a mere 89 days. A speedy trip there was rated at 115 days. McKay's ships would always do better.

McKay's ships, *Champion of the Seas*, *Flying Cloud*, *Glory of the Seas*, *Lightning*, *James Baines* and *Sovereign of the Seas*, broke record after record for speed. Even the more refined steamships could not equal their early success. The greatest of all McKay's clippers was the *Great Republic*. It was the largest wooden ship built up to its time. In the 300-foot range, it was indeed amazing. Unfortunately, it caught fire and was badly burned. With some luck, the fire was extinguished before it rendered

The American Century of Sail

Donald McKay, father of the clipper.

The Yankee Fleet

McKay's *Cornelius Grinnell* as it appeared in *Gleason's Pictorial Magazine*. Note the false gun ports painted on the side of the ship to make the vessel appear to be well armed.

the clipper irreparable. After repairs, it measured about 270 feet in length, almost 50 feet in width and was nearly 30 feet deep. It was followed by the *Donald McKay*, which was huge at 269 feet in length, 47 feet in width and was 29 feet deep. The *Donald McKay* was over 60 feet longer than the USS *Constitution*. Its cargo capacity was greater than the *Great Republic* because it was fuller in the bow and stern than other McKay clippers.

The *Donald McKay* carried 153,000 square feet of sail. That equals almost four acres of sail. It seems that the major problem of the period was finding an experienced crew to sail it. The captain, English born Henry Warner of Boston, was a grand old salt with a respectable record. He took the vessel out of Boston on February 21, 1855, on its maiden voyage with Donald McKay himself aboard. It could sail with a crew of fifty sailors, but good crewmen were hard to find in that season, and Warner had to make do with what he had, which wasn't very much as it turned out. It seems that agents had picked these not so choice men out of cheap boardinghouses and passed them off as sailors on commission. As it turned out, only eight out of the whole number had enough experience to actually climb aloft to reef sail or do any of the more difficult duties on the huge ship.

The American Century of Sail

The beautiful New York built clipper *City of Mobile* as it appeared about 1856.

Most of these recruits had been drunk on arrival and were in their bunks sick most, if not all, of the time during the maiden voyage of the *Donald McKay*. It is a most improbable bit of good fortune that the ship enjoyed some very good winds. In fact, on February 27, it made a run of 421 knots in a twenty-four-hour period. That was an average speed exceeding seventeen knots per hour. Almost no steamship could even come close to that speed in 1855. The ship made Ireland in twelve days, and it docked in Liverpool five days later. All this success with a very bad crew was a voyage to be proud of. The average crossing of the Atlantic was upwards of sixty to ninety days in the seventeenth century and about sixty to seventy days with a good wind in the eighteenth century. McKay's clippers were amazing ships. In 1787, it took Sir Arthur Phillip about six months to get from England to Australia. The *Donald McKay* did it in eighty-one days.

By the mid-1880s, the heyday of the clipper was just about over. The iron ships built by pioneers like Isambard Kingdom Brunel, who had constructed the *Great Britain* and the *Great Eastern*, showed the way to the future of commerce. Iron ships grew faster and depended less on the chance performance of the winds. The age of sail and wooden ships was truly passing. Most commerce would be carried on in steel hulls by 1900. Even most schooners and other sailing ships were now being made of steel, but at least they were still mostly powered by sail, like the giant *Thomas W. Lawson*, built in Maine. In addition to its steel construction, the Lawson had seven masts and was over 450 feet in length. Its cargo capacity was so huge that unlike wooden ships of the early twentieth century, it could compete with steam-powered vessels. But it foundered off the coast of England. At the time, it was employed as an oil tanker.

Several wooden ships lingered a few decades into the twentieth century. Whalers like the Maine built schooner *Margarett*, which slid into the sea in 1889 and had a career that lasted almost thirty years, were the last cry of the commercial sailing ship. They were beautiful to see, whether they were square-rigged or schooner-rigged. America's heart still belongs to the tall ships. In the great American Bicentennial year 1976, the tall ships sailed to Boston, Massachusetts, to mark the event of our two hundredth birthday. It was not to be the last gathering of sail. Now, I look forward to the day when the America's Cup comes back to New England where it was first exhibited in 1851. I can also dream back to the times when I used to set out under sail from the harbor of Marion, Massachusetts, with my good friend Tom Murray, now so many years ago, on that good vessel the *Broadmore*. Tom is now gone from this mortal world, but the good memories of his three decades as a master sailor are with me still as he is himself.

There is one story that has to be told before this chapter and book is through. My Uncle Bill Johnston had a remarkable and amazing father-in-law who was born in 1863. His name was John B. Hayes, and at one time or another he had done just about everything one could imagine by way of employment or business. He lived in a time in which that wide working experience was not so unusual. Most Yankee farm lads put their hand to this or that until they found what they wanted to do in life. I once knew a fellow by the name of Larnis, some fifty years ago, who said that he had stolen his profession. By that he meant that he had fallen into a profession before there were any certification requirements. And that was the way it was with John Hayes. He was a very old man of eighty-something when I used to walk up to his house on top of Forge Hill in Franklin, Massachusetts, to pass the time of day with him on his back porch listening to the transcendental and amazing stories of his life.

One of those adventures was about the time he had tried his hand at being a fisherman off the Newfoundland Banks. It is thought that English and French fishermen may have worked off the banks before the formal discovery of America and just never told anybody because they didn't want to share their treasure trove of fish with anyone else. Any good fisherman, with a favorite fishing spot, will not share the secret except maybe with his most trusted fishing buddy. I will tell you old Mr. Hayes's story just as it was related to me more than fifty years ago.

> *Well sir, I'll tell you, we were fishing off the Newfoundland Banks in '88. I know it was that year because it snowed so damn much that even New York City was buried so that nobody could move for eight days. In those days, we went in fishing for cod and mackerel. We liked firm fish, not the squishy ones like they like today* [tuna].

The American Century of Sail

John Hayes was also a dory man like this old salt pulling his lobster pot about 1888.

We were out for a long time. One day the ship was sailing along at a pretty good clip when I see the Big Swede staggering over to the ship's rail. He stands there for a minute, leans over, then he just falls overboard."

That was bad luck for the Swede I don't mind telling you, and with that, I start running down the deck yelling, "Man overboard. Man overboard." Well I ran up to the Captain and almost knocks him over, and he looks at me real mad like, and he says to me like this, "What the Hell are you going on about?"

I tell him, "The Big Swede's fallen overboard."

The Captain looks at me funny and says, "Well what the hell do you want me to do about it?"

"Shouldn't you put about sir and pick him up?" says I.

The Captain looks up at the mast and the big sail full of wind as we are going along pretty fast now. Then he turned to me and says, "No, I don't think so."

He just stares at me and goes on puffing on his pipe, and I said, "Why not? He has fallen overboard! He's going to drown for sure!"

"Yup, that's just it. By the time we put about, the Big Swede would most likely have drowned, because I know that he can't swim a lick, and he was probably drunk again anyway!" And with that, he just turned on his heel and he just walked away on down the deck puffing his pipe, and that was that.

Those old Gloucester fishermen were realists. They just don't want to pay for the same real estate twice. Times is money, and if you have no real prospect of saving somebody, sail on. Now you can't get more Yankee than that can you?

The Yankee Fleet

A schooner of the type that John Hayes sailed in off the Newfoundland Banks in 1888.

Some people kept personal journals of their voyages. Some are very dull, but every now and then a lively one like that of California gold seeker O.W. Albee comes along. Albee was a young artist from Massachusetts. He had his own portrait painted by Nahum Ball Onthank, whom I shall discuss in a bit, and it shows a young man of twenty-something with brown hair and a beard. He had blue eyes and the hint of a smile about his lips. He just looks like the sort of man who would get on a ship and travel around two continents to have an adventure that might lead to riches. Albee was very conservative in his Puritanical religious outlook, and that makes this adventure all the more interesting. Here is an extract from the journal of this refined young man showing his reaction when he is exposed to the other side of life on a little crowded ship bound for California in 1849.

> *Last evening a few of the cabin and between deck passengers* [the folks who booked the cheapest passage were the "between deck passengers" and of a lower social order] *got drunk and fought. The fight did not commence until after twelve o'clock* [midnight]. *Potter and Fox of Portland, Grover of West Cambridge, W.H. Baron of Boston, Hildreth of Boston came down to take Captain William Dire of Portland. They found him asleep so they let down a rope through the after hatch and tied it to his legs and began to draw him up, but he begged off and promised to go up and take another horn* [drink] *with them. They were all pretty well drunk then. After getting on deck, falling down a few times, drinking until they began throwing water at each other and from this to throwing off hats, caps, and tearing them in pieces or throwing them overboard. From throwing water and tearing caps, they proceeded to throw buckets of water and then they commenced a regular scuffle and fist and foot thumps. Several got sore heads and shins and all were thoroughly drenched.*

The American Century of Sail

Portrait of O.W. Albee painted by Nahum Ball Onthank in 1844 when he was only twenty-one years old and Albee was not much older.

Albee goes on, "When all lay flat on the deck squabbling, kicking, etc. some one from the roof of one of the houses threw a bucket of water and it struck Potter on the head and it cut him considerably." (I guess the fellow forgot to hold on to the bucket when he tossed the water).

Most American schoolchildren can tell you that in 1848 a man working for a Mr. Sutter found gold in the creek at Sutter's Mill, and with that, the California Gold Rush was on. The impact of this event was great. The population of California jumped from fifty thousand in 1848 to a million by 1850. Just how did all of those people get out to California in about eighteen months? Some came overland in wagon trains, but most came by ship. The Australians or "Sidney Ducks" came from the antipodes by ship across the Pacific as did Chinese and other Asians who also wanted to make a gold strike, but many more came around Cape Horn through the Strait of Magellan and up the coast of the Americas to San Francisco. There the bay was totally clogged by deserted ships, because captains, officers and crews had lit out for the California gold fields and the promise of a rich life.

Some of the abandoned ships were hauled up on to the shore and used as stores and hotels. As I stated, some years ago, I bought a portrait of the American artist O.W. Albee by the American artist Nahum Ball Onthank. Onthank was born in Massachusetts in 1823 and worked most of his professional life in Boston. He also died there in 1888 at the age of fifty-seven. Onthank had also exhibited at the Boston Athenaeum and in various important Boston Exhibitions. Onthank also exhibited in the National Academy in 1848 and in 1850. His subject, O.W. Albee, was also an artist, but more than that, he went to California in November of 1849 to make his fortune in the gold fields. We know this because Albee left that great journal of the first leg of his journey by sea to California, which I bought, along with his portrait, from David Rose of David Rose Antiques in Upton, Massachusetts.

His journal or log gives a rare insight into the life of a young Massachusetts man on the make. He was thrust into the rough-and-tumble life of a ship that was worked by some very rough and uncouth sailors who were serving aboard Albee's ship pretty much because there weren't too many qualified merchant seamen around in November and December of 1849. The reason for this was the huge number of deserters. When sailors landed in San Francisco, they took off for the gold fields only to discover that everything was taken in the way of good claims. They also discovered that food and supplies were very expensive and that it was really easy to get oneself killed without any trouble whatsoever. Shipowners had to take anybody they could get to crew their ships. Reports out of California of huge strikes of very rich gold deposits ran rampant. Easterners by the hundreds of thousands joined the million or so men who rushed to California by 1850. In fact, by that year California applied for and received statehood as the result of Henry Clay's Compromise of 1850, which placated the southern slave states and brought them into agreement.

Albee set out on his great adventure on November 29, 1849, but he would not board the ship until the next day, which was a Saturday. Then he would have to wait until

The American Century of Sail

Albee's log of his voyage to California.

December 4 to depart from Boston. He hated the long wait on the good ship Cheshire. On Sunday, the ship had left the "T" Wharf and anchored in the channel because a northeaster was blowing up. It didn't seem a lucky start to the voyage. Albee writes, "We were obliged to lie in the stream until Wednesday until half past eleven A. M. when the pilot came on board and we hoisted sail. In a few minutes we were under way. The pilot took us to the outer light and then left the ship to Captain Dix of Portland."

Albee then writes,

> *The breeze was fair and the captain put on the sail. We went ahead at a spanking rate, passed the Nauset light at four o'clock in the evening. Weather rather cloudy with*

> *a stiff breeze. I need not speak of the feelings which came welling up at each point. Leaving home, losing sight of Boston, and lastly of every speck of Massachusetts soil and launching out into the broad Atlantic. Those feelings can more easily be imagined than described. Probably every son of New England experienced nearly the same as I did.*

Like every young man setting out on a first major voyage, Albee was homesick. It was cold, but soon he would be in warmer latitude, which was a good thing on a sailing ship. It was also fortunate that whereas the northern hemisphere was on the verge of winter, the southern hemisphere was about to enjoy summer.

Albee went on to discuss the seasickness of many aboard the *Cheshire*. This included the pigs, which were the first affected by the movement of the ship. Albee writes, "The pigs on board were the first taken and the manner they were led, bent up their backs and gagged and staggered was laughable to look upon, and offered amusement to many a two legged creature that were soon to go through with conditions very similar to the pigs."

Albee did not approve of the ungodly conduct of most of the crew who seemed to enjoy the extreme discomfort of Albee and the rest of the landlubbers. They decried the praying of the Yankees until they reached the stormy waters of Cape Horn and the terrible trials of the Strait of Magellan. Things hadn't been so easy up to that point. Albee reports in his journal,

> *One of the seamen called out, "Don't you see any danger standing there? Don't you see that everything is torn to the Devil above you." So I stepped into the midship and took a view of the destruction. The squall which had struck the ship at daybreak tore in flitters the fore top sail, one of the largest sails in the ship. Broke in the middle of the fore top yard was a timber about 30 feet long and nine inches through at the place where it broke. It split the mizzen top sail from top to bottom. This is another big sail. So you see the squall did pretty thorough execution and we who are here in the business of voyaging upon the stormy ocean felt we had a fair introduction to begin with.*

Bad weather continued for the better part of a couple of weeks. The winds played havoc with the rigging, and by December 12, Albee was told that the ship had made about 1,500 miles. He writes, "I have been pretty well...and am thoroughly drenched."

Albee is disillusioned with the character of most of his companions. He writes,

> *The gamblers are at it early this morning before breakfast, and one fellow lost the little he had. They gambled most of the night. Yesterday by request I drew up a Constitution for a debating club. About 40 signed it. But I doubt much the success of the effort. Last evening Mr. White and another gentleman made a phrenological*

A highly idealized print of the port of Portsmouth, New Hampshire, as seen from Kittery Bridge in 1875.

> *examination of several heads* [phrenology was the study of bumps on a person's head, which was made to tell what the future might hold, popular as a pseudoscience at the time] *to which they affixed various characteristics.*

The next day the debating club was organized. Albee also was interested in the fact that the ship had been insured as a temperance ship. He thought that odd with the drinking going on. He wondered what the rates would be to insure the *Cheshire* as an antitemperance ship. He also records other ships seen among them such as an English bark, a full-rigged ship and a Danish West Indian ship bound for home.

Recalling that drunken fight Albee witnessed that I related earlier, I'm sure that by the time he got to San Francisco, some of the culture shock had worn off. San Francisco was a lawless city where justice, such as it was, was a vigilante system with a certain quality of inexactness about it. Just who got hanged and who didn't was largely a question of the perception of the day and the luck of the draw.

Like a lot of lucky folks who went to the gold fields after surviving the trip around the Horn, Albee came, he saw and he didn't strike it rich, but he did get to tell about it, which a lot of his contemporaries did not. Toward the end of his journal, which would make a pretty interesting book, he writes these philosophical and not so oddly familiar lines.

The Yankee Fleet

What the Sea Can Do, a circa 1875 print that indicates the fate of the great vessels at the End of the era of the ironmen and wooden ships.

> *Those golden dreams of ours have burst*
> *And left us humbled in the dust*
> *We are here at last and find it true*
> *Minus gold; tremendous blue.*
> *We'll turn our steps towards that lot,*
> *Where stands our lowly humble cot*
> *And spend our days in pleasure there*
> *To build no castles in the air.*

The Albee journal is written in a schoolbook called *The Young Composer*, which is a textbook about how to write compositions written by Charles Northend of Portland and published by Sanborn and Carter in 1848. It is inscribed:

Mr. O.W. Albee
With the respects of Chas. Northend.

Mr. Northend must have given his friend Albee a couple of these composition books with their numerous blank pages to be used on his voyage to the gold fields. I know that there is a least one more notebook yet unaccounted for, with the rest of Albee's story in it. Look about for it on your rambles around the bookshops of New England before most, or even all, of those shops are gone forever.

So many good friends, who like myself were in love with the sea and the world of books, are gone now, like Tom Murray who introduced me to sailing thirty years ago and Donald Howes of Brewster who always had a treasure of great old books that could be found nowhere else for me to peruse each time I visited him. I am sure that most of you reading this little book about the sea and the ships that sailed upon it share the love of history that embraces us lucky folks who live in New England. This is a place rich in history and the wonderful artifacts of our sea-influenced past. Our blood has about all the elements found in seawater in it. I think that is the vital factor that binds us to this mystic shore. The great Atlantic is in our blood, and in a way, it is our mother. From the sea our ancestors came, and before I journey to that far away country from which no soul returns, my last thoughts will be about my sailing on those wide waters just beyond the Cape that I have always loved so well.

Bibliography

Albee, O.W. *Journal to California By Way of Cape Horn.* 1849–1850.

Andrist, Ralph K. *History of the Making of the Nation.* New York: American Heritage Publishing Co., 1969.

Arnold, D.C. *Official Views of the World's Columbian Exposition.* Chicago: Press Chicago Photogravure Co., 1893.

Beetle, Henry Hough. *The New England Story.* New York: Random House, 1958.

Botta, Charles. *History of the War of Independence of the United States of America.* New York: T. Brainaid, 1839.

Bowditch, Nathaniel. *The New American Practical Navigator.* New York: E. and G.W. Blunt, 1837.

Brewington, M.V. *The Peabody Collection of Navigating Instruments.* Salem: Peabody Museum, 1963.

Bryant, Sir Arthur. *The Age of Chivalry.* New York: New American Library, 1963.

———. *Celebration of the Two Hundred and Fiftieth Anniversary of the Settlement of Boston.* Boston: The City Council, 1880.

Chapelle, Howard I. *The Charters and General Laws of the Colony and Province of Massachusetts Bay.* Boston: The General Court, 1814.

Bibliography

———. *The History of the American Sailing Navy.* New York: Bonanza Books, 1949.

Cheever, George. *The Journal of the Pilgrims.* New York: John Wiley, 1849.

Clark, Thomas H., and Colin Stearn. *The Geological Evolution of North America.* New York: Ronald Press Co., 1960.

Dana, Richard Henry. *Two Years Before the Mast.* New York: Viking Press, 2003.

Davis, Andrew McFarland. *Tracts Relating to the Currency of the Massachusetts Bay.* Boston: Houghton, Mifflin and Company, 1902.

Drake, Samuel Adams. *Nooks and Corners of the New England Coast.* New York: Harper and Brothers, 1875.

———. *Old Landmarks and Historic Personages of Boston.* Boston: James R. Osgood and Company, 1873.

Drake, Samuel G. *History and Antiquities of Boston.* Boston: Luther Stevens, 1856.

Duydkinck, Evert. *History of the World.* New York: Johnson, Fry, and Co., 1869.

Ellet, Mrs. E.F. *Court Circles of the Republic.* Hartford: Hartford Publishing Company, 1869.

———. *Encyclopedia of Massachusetts: Biographical and Genealogical.* New York: The American Historical Society Inc., 1895.

Esquemeling, John. *The Buccaneers of America.* New York: Charles Scribner's Sons, 1898.

Forbes, Esther. *Paul Revere and the World He Lived in.* Boston: Houghton, Mifflin, 1942.

Foreman, Henry Chandler. *Early Nantucket and Its Whale Houses.* New York: Hastings House, 1966.

Freuchen, Peter. *Peter Freuchen's Book of the Seven Seas.* New York: Julian Messner, Inc., 1957.

Gibbon, Edward. *The Decline and Fall of the Roman Empire.* New York: The Publishers' Plate Renting Co., 1890.

Bibliography

Griffiths, John W. *The Ship Builder's Manual and Nautical Referee.* New York: John W. Griffiths, 1853.

Harper's Magazine, 1858, 1860, 1877, 1878, 1890, 1894, 1896, 1900, 1904, 1905.

Hawksworth, John. *A New Voyage Around the World.* New York: James Rivington, 1774.

Hawthorne, Daniel. *Ships of the Seven Seas.* New York: Garden City Publishing, 1925.

Higginson, Thomas Wentworth. *Young Folk's History of the United States.* Boston: Lee and Shepard, 1879.

Isaacson, Walter. *Benjamin Franklin: An American Life.* New York: Simon and Schuster, 2003.

Johnson, Charles. *A General History of the Robberies and Murders of the Most Notorious Pirates.* Boston: n.p., 1724.

Kane, Elisha Kent. *Artic Explorations.* Philadelphia: Child's and Peterson, 1856.

King, Moses. *King's Handbook of Boston.* Cambridge: Moses King, 1878.

Krause, Chester L. *World Coins.* Iola, KS: Krause Publishing Co., 2006.

Lippincott, Bertram. *Indians, Privateers, and High Society.* Philadelphia: J.B. Lippincott Company, 1961.

Longacre, James. *National Portrait Gallery of Distinguished Americans.* Philadelphia: James Kay Jr. and Brother, 1836.

Marsh, Edward. *North American Indians.* London: The Aboriginies Committee, 1844.

McCullough, David. *1776.* New York: Simon and Schuster, 2005.

Melville, Herman. *Billy Budd.* New York: Limited Editions Club, 1965.

———. *Moby Dick.* New York: Barnes and Noble, 2005. First published 1851 by Harper & Brothers.

Morris, Paul C. *American Sailing Coasters of North America.* New York: Bonanza Books, 1973.

Bibliography

Morse, Jedidiah. *Geography Made Easy.* Boston: Thomas Andrews, 1807.

Nutting, Wallace. *Massachusetts Beautiful.* New York: Bonanza Books, 1949.

———. *Ocean Scenes.* Leavitt and Allen, 1855.

Oppel, Frank. *Tales of Old New England.* Edison, NJ: Castle Books, 1986.

Philip, U. *Lost Greenland.* New York: Harper and Brothers, 1844.

Poore, Ben Perley. *Perley's Reminiscences.* Philadelphia: Hubbard Brothers, 1886.

———. *Punch or the London Charivari.* London: Bradbury, Agnew, and Company, 1874.

Pyle, Howard. *Howard Pyle's Book of Pirates.* New York: Charles Scribner's Sons, 1921.

Robotti, Frances Diane. *Chronicles of Old Salem.* New York: Bonanza Books, 1948.

Russell, Francis. *Adams: An American Dynasty.* New York: American Heritage Publishing Co., 1976.

Smith, John. *The Generall Historie of Virginia, New England, and the Summer Isles.* London: Michael Sparkes, 1624.

Smith, Page. *Jefferson: A Revealing Biography.* New York: American Heritage Publishing Co., 1976.

Snell, Captain Moses. *Journal of a Voyage Onboard the Ship Archer of New Bedford Bound to the Indian Ocean and North West Coast.* 1845–1847.

Suetonius, Gaius Tranquillius. *The Lives of the Twelve Emperors of Rome.* New York: Heritage Press, 1965.

Thomas, Isaiah. *Almanacs.* Worcester, MA: Isaiah Thomas, 1799–1827.
Trowbridge, Captain Asa F. *The Log of the Ship Canada.* 1877.

———. *The Log of the Voyage of the Ship Edith.* 1874-1875.

Upham, Charles W. *Salem Witchcraft.* Boston: Wiggan and Lunt, 1867.

Bibliography

Verril, A. Hyatt. *The Real Story of the Whaler.* New York: D. Appleton and Company, 1916.

Weems, John Edward. *The Fate of the Maine.* New York: Henry Holt and Company, 1958.

Williams, Harold. *One Whaling Family.* Boston: Houghton Mifflin Company, 1964.

Visit us at
www.historypress.net